Clowns & Silver Balls

D Everett Newell

ISBN: 978-81-19654-41-3

First Edition: 2024
Rs. 200/-

Cyberwit.net
HIG 45 Kaushambi Kunj, Kalindipuram
Allahabad - 211011 (U.P.) India
http://www.cyberwit.net
Tel: +(91) 9415091004
E-mail: info@cyberwit.net

Printed at Repro India Limited.

DEDICATION

This book, "Clowns & Silver Balls",

This will be my 12th book of mostly original, non-published writings since I started in 2006.

My thanks always to Judy "J" Elder, my editor and board to bounce ideas off of.

My thanks to my publisher Cyberwit.net. The last twenty years they have made it easy.

I want to thank my family - my wife and friend Kathy Newell, and my parents John and Dorothy Newell.

I want to thank all my friends and co-workers, classmates, who I have known through the years. You have lived in and between all the pages of my writings.

It is always my hope that I have left a measure of who I am and have been as a man and person in my writings. My intent is to allow future generations to know me somewhat, if they would want to.

I have re-invented myself many times now, in a lifespan of almost 71 years. I imagine I will keep doing that till the end! I'm still 18 at heart!

Lastly, I need to give thanks to these most important people, who by their lives keep me living mine. I love you Corey Everett Newell, Alissa Angeline (Newell) Staats, Nakoa Christopher Staats, Saige Corey Newell, Shawnee Angeline Staats, Ella Lynn Newell, Maddox Everett Staats. Thank You all from the bottom of my heart!

Thanks also to my son-in-law Rodney Staats, and my daughter-in-law Jamie Newell.

A special Thank You to Doug Hodges who once again helped me write one more saga with Bob!

A special Thank You to MY RATPACK TRAVELING Group. You own a piece of my HEART!

Thank You to Zach "Noodles" Newell, he is our family's next great Wordsmith!

Thanks again to Doug Hodges my mentor, Judy Wolford Pierannunzio my Dear Friend!

This Book is Dedicated and in Remembrance to: These very Special people!

Lou Furino

Jo DeLancey

And My Mom, Dorothy Irene Newell,

I promise you will never be Forgotten!

Anyway, A mighty Thanks to you all!

As always, I remain humbly yours

The Big D

D Everett Newell

THE AUTHOR, D EVERETT NEWELL

My name is Dennis Everett Newell; I am called in no certain order, Denny, Den, Big D, D Everett, and Dennis. It's funny, but I can usually tell by how someone calls my name, what time in my life we shared. I guess there are many layers to a life that has now spanned almost 71 years. My middle name, Everett, has been passed down in our family since the Civil War. My great-great-grandfather's name was Darius Newell, who named his son Silas Everett Newell, my great-grandfather. He in turn named his son John Everett Newell, my grandfather, who then in turn named my dad, John Everett Newell Jr. My dad named me Dennis Everett Newell, and my son is Corey Everett Newell, and my great-grandson Maddox Everett Staats.

Poetry and my stories are my way of slaying the inner dragons within my mind, thus allowing my inner feelings and passions to escape – my relief valve if you will! I draw on my own personal inspiration from my assimilations and experience of my life lived. Experiences that I have taken then shaped and formed into stories and poems. Moments garnered from all people I have interacted with, during all these years of living. I am from a family with a long history of wordsmiths. Within these pages, I try not to let down those that came before me, and to pass a standard to those who will come after. Taking on this family mantle, I do so with pride and to the best of my meager abilities.

I now live in Western New York, an area that if you don't like the weather, wait 24 hours and it will change. The people that live here are tough, able, caring and resilient. I originated from the hills of Pennsylvania - a small town, Falls Creek, in the foothills of the Allegheny Mountain chain. Within my family heritage you will find lumberjacks, coal miners, and people of every vocation. You will also find warmth, loyalty and support. This family is the most loving and lovely family a young boy and now late middle-aged man could possibly ever hope for.

My passions are, in no particular order, writing, photography, paranormal, history (Civil War and WW II), music, poetry, sports, computers, and I am a people watcher. I am you see, an eclectic spirit, hence these eclectic thoughts. I hope with all of my heart, something you read in this book will touch you. I hope you can pause and maybe reflect on your own life and world. My Dad taught me very early on, be a 'stop and smell the roses' man!

Thank YOU.

D Everett Newell, the Big D

To reach the Big D, his email is Bygd1@aol.com,

You can find all 12 of my books for purchase on Amazon, Cyberwit.Net, or by emailing me personally

Contents

16 Million Tears

They were willing to give all
Seventeen or eighteen years of age
Lifting the whole world on their shoulders
Many would die, never to return home
The ones that did, paid a huge cost
Never again were they the same
That generation was more somber, stoic
Laughed a little less, cried a bit more
Nervous systems mostly used up
Saving our country, our way of life
Setting most people everywhere free
Doing what they had to do
Never questioning as they volunteered
En mass they moved, on to Europe
On to Japan, many horrors seen
Now they are leaving us
So many now gone, the rest
Ancient by today's standard
Frail mostly, but still a gleam
Bright sparks left in their eyes
In the very, very least
These men & women shed 16 million tears
We were lucky they were here!

D Everett Newell 11/18/2022

Dedicated to my Dad and the 16 million men & women Who Saved The Free World During WWII They are shrinking into history!

A Conduit

The paper stares back at me
Being on a roll, I won't be stopped
Words usually pour from somewhere
Turning on the spigot, OK
Nothing, maybe message my brain
Think wondrous thoughts, surely that works
Waiting, still nothing, seems my line
From somewhere in the universe
Is plugged, an idea, I'll plunge it
Waiting, watching, waiting, watching
Pick up my pen, muscle memory engages
Slowly I see ink on paper
Smiling, I'm getting somewhere
Like a printer with new ink
Flowing now, ideas forced down
Brilliant, possibly, passable
I hope, the very least interesting
I'll await feedback
When this piece is finished
Thankful, whatever this is
Is, and I'm allowed access
I'm a conduit from somewhere
To your heart, mind and souls

D Everett Newell 5/6/2022

A Gift For all who read my Pieces!
Let me know if you get it?

The Most Beautiful Poem Ever

I long ago was told
Poetry is a painted picture
A photo in the reader's mind
A story that evokes emotion
I've always tried to do that
Here today I'm taking it further
As you read my words
Stop, close your eyes
Open your mind and soul
Now visualize the most stunning
The prettiest, indescribable vision
You have ever come across
Think deep, it's in there
We all see things and
Experience events, people
Music, all in different ways
Now after you've done this
I ask, did I live up to
My promise, did you experience
And see the most beautiful sight
You ever experienced
Making this the most
Beautiful poem ever!

D Everett Newell 7/26/2022

You're Welcome!

Whining About Pictures

You've heard of wine
With your delicious cheese
Well, all I get is
Whine with taking pictures
Every day we are as good
As we will ever be
I try to capture my
Friends and family forever
In an unending series of photos
Real life stuff, not posed
Any more all I get
Is a referendum, a chorus
Of delete this, delete that
I stand my ground
Amidst a myriad of threats
Voluminous at times, but I
Hold steady, finger on the button
Why take one, when
Ten more will do
Sending us all to the
Dustbin of memories, whereby
People in our futures will see
How cool we were, so please
Quit whining about pictures

D Everett Newell 6/30/2023

A Rainy Day

It's a gray day
Wet, windy, wild
God's creatures gone
Hiding in protection
Staying dry, comfortable
Trees drinking, swaying
What was brown
You see turning green
This nocturnal world
Moods become dark
Too much time
To reflect and think
It's June and I know
The sun is not far away
Tomorrow will be lighter
So will I, brighter
Funny how things
Affect we humans
We're not separated
From nature, no
Always a part of it
God's plan connects us
And our peach on earth

D Everett Newell 6/16/2023

A thought last night in my sleep, about how we're faced with change constantly!

I'm Adjustable

I awaken eight AM in the morning
Cozy the sunlight hits me
Time to arise, fight another day
That is OK, very doable
For you see, I'm adjustable
The phone rings unexpectedly a friend
Hey, want to come out and play
The day's plan changes on a whim
That is OK, very doable
For you see, I'm adjustable
The meal we were having up in smoke
Charred beyond recognition moving on
We order take-out a place near us
That is OK, very doable
For you see, I'm adjustable
The national news makes me cry
Turning it off and my music on
My mood lightens smiling again
That is OK, very doable
For you see, I'm adjustable
Another day put to rest sleepily
Move to bedroom and prepare to lay down
Achy sore joints hurt but
That is OK, very doable
For you see, I'm adjustable

D Everett Newell 7/12/2023

A Time, A Place

As I turned the Bluetooth on
Music from yesterday played
50 Years from my past, it came
Memories sprouted up instantly
I see in my mind's eye, all of it
A time, a place, who I was with
Knowing I should be glad, I shed a tear
Why, I know not, salty moisture shed
It was the best time of my life
Young, unencumbered with pain, free
I came and went as I wanted
Little to no life responsibilities
Honestly, I knew then it was special
I tried to drink it all in
Every drop of the sweet elixir of life
I've lived a good life, no complaints
Great wife, wonderful family, great friends, Yet,
When the songs and the memories leave
A small hole remains in my heart
The faces I just saw are erased
My eyes clear from the salted irritated red
Memories are a double-edged sword
As I turned the Bluetooth on
Music from yesterday played
50 Years from my past, it came

D Everett Newell 1/4/2024

A Tree Named Bruce

'Wood' you be mine
I asked a blue spruce
He said, No, you're allergic
But, in any event my name is Bruce

We agreed to disagree
Bruce and I
Hugged as we parted
Tears and redness in my eyes

On my way home
Alone and thinking to myself
To tree or not to tree
Nay, I'll put up an elf on a shelf

Thus ends this little poem
One about this big guy and Bruce
Did not know where it was going
Now is the time to end this post

'Wood' you be mine
Again, I ask a blue spruce
The answer once more, No
But remember me, a tree named Bruce

D Everett Newell 12/1/2021

AABCDFFSY

Aerodrome, a landing field
Alienism, treatment of mental illness
Brabble, to squabble or quarrel
Charabanc, a wagon with benches
Deliciate, to amuse or please oneself
Frigorific, causing cold or is chilling
Frutescent, an appearance of a shrub
Supererogation, advanced form of interrogation
Younker, a young man or a child
So, what have I written about?
This my memoriam on these nine
Nine words erased from our
English dictionary, so let us
Never forget them!

D Everett Newell 1/6/2022

Adopt Don't Shop

We were so excited
The car pulled into our property
A new hope came with it
One of us getting a new home
This Rescue has been wonderful
Yet, I yearn for a place of my own
A family to love, play with
One to grow old with
In this moment I'm hopeful
I drop the ball I'm playing with
Our Human mother seems happy
Which usually is a pretense of good
Tails wagging, and our crew running
To and fro, jumping playfully
Rolling, jumping with excitment
Are they are looking my way
Oh my God, they are
Now walking in my direction
I must present my best self
My heart skipping beats
Please, please, Pick Me, Pick me
I feel their hands around me,
Then I am turned around
Checking my body over
Like some cheap door prize
Something is off, only coldness emits
Setting me back down, a frown
Walking away, nodding "No"
I pick up my toy and retreat

Sitting now in a corner
My head down, a small tear
The tilt of joy for now is gone
The car drives away
Again I wonder when
Please adopt don't shop

D Everett Newell 2/17/2022

All About Lists

Life, it's all about lists
You know, the rungs on your ladder
As you have ascended life
Looking back holding on tightly
Fighting to move higher
Doing so with determination and confidence
Clouds come into focus as you go
But no worry, they will dissipate
Little embers of mist cast aside
Like the puff ball in your back yard
One strong wind and mysteriously gone
Climbing on is what we do
As if pre-programmed,
We are not stationary
Born to assimilate, to experience
Then we record and remember
Passing down our trek to others
As I stated, we somehow
Make it through
Life is all about lists

D Everett Newell 5/26/2023

All Possibilities, All Concerns

At my age, late sixties
My life is full, loving family
Many upon many great friends
Let me talk to my fur family
We have two older girls
Their time to leave draws near
We will love and care for them
Until they go over the rainbow bridge
We have a little love of three
Dilemmas demand long sincere thought
I don't want our Zoey
To go through life without another girl
One to share her life with
But it's a real probability
Our next puppy may outlive us
Am I being greedy to not promise
A protection and care through that life?
I ponder this, have to examine
All possibilities, all concerns

D Everett Newell 1/25/2022

Anatomy

We dissect all living creatures
Every man, every woman, every child
Moving on to the animal kingdom
Followed by the vast insect world
Doing so to find an understanding
To define what life is
What is this mystical wonderful thing
Let us not forget the plants
Who feed us all, nurturing our growth
This world is a jigsaw of moving parts
So vast, so ridiculous to grasp
But we try, God knows we try
Ironic our God does know
A beautiful world, let us
Try not to screw it up
Just enjoy it as it plays out
One bit at a time we see
Developing before our eyes
This wonderful anatomy!

D Everett Newell 5/26/2023

Answers are Fleeting

Sometimes not comfortable
Living in today's world
Internet, cell phones, 4K TV's
Sure, I have info at a touch
But at times, I'd like to tap out
Life is quicker, with more stress
A video game with too many players
I can't keep up most days
Providing a sense that each morning
I'm further behind
There are moments
Things slow down
Way too infrequent to be any measure
I'm always waking and going to bed
Most of the time in between, not memorable
In fact, robotic, automatic patterns
Not really living a life, my life
Just playing one on TV
An actor doing and following a script
Is it my story I'm playing?
At times, I do wonder
Guess I will never totally understand
Oh well, for now I'll keep probing
Answers are fleeting at best

D Everett Newell 1/28/2022

Artisan

Once upon a time in a land far far away
One made the cheese
Here lived an Artisan,
Cutting one piece at a time
Aged as it was, filled with aroma
He was very succinct with his edges
Each package, one after another
Weighed the same
All day, all night, dispatching to the world
Many trucks enroute to all corners
Precisely at dawn he started
Sleeping only six hours from full moon
Till the sun rose on the plain again
You'd think he'd be a very rich person
But no, living paycheck to paycheck
Much as we common people do
Wake up, work, then to bed once more
His wealth was measured within himself
In a knowledge his job was well done
A lot can be said about giving full measure
Some try to cheat life at times
Getting by, doing nothing, letting
Others take the worries, the work
Is that a life worth living?
Simply said, an integral passage of time
Amounts to more than those people think
No real point or astounding moral
I'm here to tell and I'm telling plainly
Read what you will, take out what you will
Again, one more time, I repeat
Once upon a time in a land far far away
One made the cheese

D Everett Newell 7/15/2023

As a Poet

As a poet, as a writer
I get asked often
Could you write about anything?
Just post a subject, and go
Something asked of me
By you to tackle
I suppose, if I had an interest,
Coupled with some passion
I'd try, but do not usually
My pieces are not scripted
What comes to me is free flowing
From where, I do not always know
Just there for me to decipher
I never question what I'm given
The idea appears, forms, takes flight
Seeing a snapshot in my mind
Then I tell that particular story
Hoping to draw others in
Hoping to evoke feelings, emotions
A painting of words if you will
Never can I fix all that ills
Or our worlds many problems
Wish upon wish I might
What I can do is make you think
Pause upon your hectic lives
Smile, cry, sometimes both
My success lies solely,
Truly upon your traveled worn feet
Your heart and souls,

Hold the keys to decipher
Being a conduit of such
Doing my best, in this quest
My only hope, is you
As it is always the singular reader
Finds meaning in my literary canvases

D Everett Newell 4/13/2022

Ashes to Ashes

Watching the last moments of my parents' lives
Albeit thirty-three years apart, seems like yesterday
Their love, ideals, memories, awash in death's shroud
Tore at my heart, denting my soul
Realizing I'm now the last line of family defense
I'll carry on, I must, as they did for all who come after
Dad always said, we start dying the day we're born
So very hard those last goodbyes
Each asked that I take them home, I could not
Each time changed me
Each time a little piece of me went with them
Ashes to ashes my royal loves
My King and Queen will always live within me
I'll never quit seeing you in my dreams
Hearing your concerned, teaching voices
I'm so thankful for the time we did share
Of course, I wanted more
Sleep well
Goodnight
Goodbye
Missing you
You'll aways be for me
Loyal steadfast
Pillars of love & support

D Everett Newell 3/4/2022

I Love you Dorothy Irene Carr Newell, and John Everett Newell JR, you made me a very lucky Kid

Assumptions

Judging people can be disastrous
Without facts or backgrounds
Making assumptions, of knowing
When we really don't, leads us
To many bad decisions
Refrain from trying to understand
The various actions of others
Turn the other cheek, hand out
The multiple chances to all
As we would want done to us
So many times in life
Friendships are lost because we
Think one thing, and we are wrong
I think back on my life
Wishing I could reclaim my losses
People in some way I hurt
Because I crossed that middle line
Causing a relationship accident
By judging people without facts
Making my assumptions
That made an ass of me
Not you!

D Everett Newell 11/2/2022

Avalanche

Feelings rushed in
Quickly, demanding notice
The exact moment
Our eyes met
Something in the way
You looked at me
Something in the way
You move
Feeling a flushing warmth
Taking me off guard
Wow I think, what was that
Can't wait now, until we meet again
Heart and stomach flutters
Every time you're near
Is this a sickness
Attractions work this way
And when cared for
They grow into friendships
Sometimes into love lasting
A lifelong coupling, a
Do or die symbiotic partnership
My soul is on fire
My destiny seeable, I'm ready
For this avalanche of love

D Everett Newell 1/7/2022

For Love wherever however you can find it

Bangs the Gong

Do you hear the noise
An alarm to awaken
Time for all good people
To stand for each other
Strip away religions
All corrupt governments
All we have left is us
Each of us a unicorn
So unique,
Never will another
Like us come this way
Spread warmth and love
With all that you do
Fight for the downtrodden
The underdogs need a prop up
In doing so, lifting ourselves up
We are predestined in ways
Not understood, to help others
Doing that our own memorial
Our stories,
Get passed through generations
Everlasting life comes from doing good
Don't let despair, disenchantment
Become barriers too big that they stop us
Moral agents are that army
That loudly bangs the Gong

D Everett Newell 6/12/2023

Beach

Running into the ocean
Splishing, splashing the water
Broad wide grin of fun
Gleefully playing like an otter

Water glistens, beads, drops
Skin shines from sun's shine
Cares are lifted away
This good time will always be mine

Sand at my feet, a slight burn
Shifting as I step, then covering
Subtle changes, a delight
My day at the beach gets me right

Birds playing among the waves
Sand piper trotting along the shore
Clouds passing creates shadows
Contrasts that enrich, leaves me wanting more

D Everett Newell 1/6/2022

Ocean pacifies me, its clean simple, like this poem

Beaten

Woke up early this morn
I feel tired and beaten
My stomach growls then moans
As if an army marches inside
On against my will, my fight interrupted
Feeling hopeless as of now
Anyone else have days like this?
Please offer up remedies
Help me smile and feel light
Oh, I know this is a temporary state
But the weight drags on me
Bends my spine, leaving me winded
Trying to move on, hour by hour
Waiting on days end, then start anew
Hoping tomorrow starts more complete
I wish these days would hide unto themselves
Thankful they don't last long
Or occur in a more frequent rotation
Still, it gets my attention
Wanting to know why on some days
I feel so beaten!

D Everett Newell 10/6/2022

Beautiful

Beautiful is a starry Christmas Eve
Beautiful is all of the holiday music
Beautiful are all of the dreams before
Beautiful is getting up with anticipation
Beautiful is the blue of light snow
Beautiful is seeing kids' faces
Beautiful is the giving of love
Beautiful is the wonders of the day
Beautiful is the gathering of people
Beautiful is the bountiful dinners
Beautiful is the games played
Beautiful is that restful sleep
Beautiful are memories created forever

It is not the money spent
Always, it's the people who care
Friend and family create magic
And it is always beautiful

D Everett Newell 12/7/2022

Being That Friend

If a friend is needed
Try and be steadfast
When you talk, surely I will listen
No opinions offered
Unless one is asked for
Sometime a shoulder is wanted
Nothing else, support is simple
Lend heart, soul, and ears
Hear a person's story
Let it unfold naturally
No forcing, prodding, expecting
Don't take it personally, ever
If conversations are slow
Basic rule, a hard one
Just be there, be human
Knowing time cures all ills
Silent confidence bolsters us all
Camaraderie shields us, simply said
You can show love
By being patient and consistent
Building credibility that cements
Just by being that friend

D Everett Newell 12/10/2022

Better Tomorrows

Done writing for the day
I was blank left pondering
Feeling rather mundane
Then in this moment
A late entry came to me
As I sat gazing out
The gray clouds parted
The sun shone down
For a brief moment, clarity
Giving me hope
Looking toward a future
Needing to use rose-tinted glasses
I must believe in our tomorrows
Will be brighter than our todays
Knowing every day is a gift
I do remain humble, thankful
Yet, don't blame me for wanting
I'd love to see more love
I'd love to have all experience peace
I'd love to not deal with hate
I'd love to have true equality
For all my brothers and sisters
To enjoy some unbridled happiness
To end all senseless killings
To end all senseless wars
To end petty jealousy and division
For all of mankind to hold hands
Every people of every nation
Stripped of religion, political bias

Of the governments that betray them
The world is made up of mostly good
Yes, good decent hard-working people
Here I sit, describing all that's good or bad
Looking, praying for better tomorrows

D Everett Newell 4/14/2022

Big Brother

Government's new mandates
Are a dogma of endless intrusions
Knowing all we do, the new mantra
Well, go on, bring it on
I mean, my life is so exciting
Getting up, I eat breakfast
Well, after I stumble to the kitchen
Then, I take a fistful of meds
After which, I help dispose
Another fistful of pills to
Our loving but elderly doggies
I may write a bit, possibly
If voice allows, record a podcast
Then I heat up my lunch
Following that with coffee, more meds
I pee a lot, so that is breaking news
So now I need more water
Doing dishes, straightening the kitchen
Tasks to excite, then maybe
Listen to music or watch TV
On crazy days, I do both
Then plan and eat supper
Settling in 'til bedtime, I'm exhausted
Sleeping and waking the next day
To start all over again
I forgot to mention all the wealth
Acquired and hidden in my secret caches
So much for my communist plot
There you have it, Big Brother

D Everett Newell 12/14/2021

Billy

Growing up in the very quiet
Very, very, small town
Falls Creek, PA
We had safety,
And our vivid imaginations
Simpler times, but we created
Games, of sport, competition,
Both physical and of mind
Clusters of kids my age
Got together at every chance
Daylight to dusk, every day an adventure
This is about one of those kids
Billy, at the time, was very friendly
Five-ten, 180 pounds, with a beard
You see, our Billy, years earlier
Had been hurt, severely injured
He was now, forevermore, a child
One in a man's body,
But still a child
Now as far as I recollect
None of my peers treated him differently
Looking back now, I'm sure
Parents, as I would be,
Were a bit apprehensive
Still, Billy was a part of our lives
Memories of him walking the town
Pulling a little red wagon
Picking Blueberries and
Picking up any bottles lying about

This was Billy's job
He did this most of his life
I recently heard from a friend
Billy had died a while back
But until he did, led his life
To his best ability
I'm sure when he got
To the gates in Heaven
He and his blue stained hands,
And his red wagon in tow
The pearly gates swung quickly open
This little town that cradled his life
Forevermore hold him in remembrance
With a now annual Red Wagon Campaign
To help people of need
I to this day and into the future
Will remember our friend, Bill

D Everett Newell 12/1/2021

Bit Saddened

I'm a bit saddened today
Not one to like change
Cringing with each new wrinkle
To a life I've known
A life I've grown accustomed to
Yesterday came the news
Another local landmark is closing
Sunset Drive-In, Middleport, NY
I first met you long ago
1967 the year, I saw "Valley of the Dolls"
Partly my fault, as I frequent less
As distance and life's treadmill
Consumed me most weeks
Reflecting now, so many nights
Sitting under the stars as a kid
Then High School summers with my friends
Drinking, talking, kissing, oh and the movies
Chapters with you came and went
Time with my kids, family, and
Older friends, your french-fries
Submarine sandwiches legendary
Now can't believe you'll be gone
I'm a bit saddened today!

D Everett Newell 1/13/2022

BOGO

BOGO, a paradox at times
Buy one, get one free
The sign reads
Simple enough I think
Then seeing the smaller print
Buy one full sub, then
Get one half sub free
Really, is this the spirit of…
Or is this a ghost of, BOGO past?
You never see, buy one car
Get another at same value free
Or a house, or anything
Of real value, make a difference value
So, I'm writing this
At my own free will
Stating, buy this poem
I'll write another free
See, BOGO is real to me

D Everett Newell 12/13/2021

Bologna

I can taste it now
The meat we grew up with
One songs were written about
Many a school lunch captured it
Two slices of white bread
A generous dab of yellow mustard
To fancy it up, slice of American cheese
On rare occurrence, fry it in a pan
Eat with peppers or onions
My all-time favorite peppers in oil
A meat made of cow pieces
Set to jell, then sliced
Sounds wonderful, doesn't it?
Surprisingly good, a salty heaven
A wonder the bar set so low
Americans grew up with it
The caviar of the working poor
Only other alternative was the old
Peanut butter and jelly, but don't
Get me started on that, for another time
Let's rejoice, let's be thankful
For our choice of this versatile meat
I hope I've spurred your appetite
Now repeat, I say repeat after me
B O L O G N A!

D Everett Newell 7/17/2023

Bonfire

Line up the wood
Get it started, slowly
Hear that sharp cracking, hissing
Building to that crescendo of
Flame smoke and heat
Somehow in this destruction
We find calm, a peace
Really amazing how that works
Nothing better than sitting around
A blaze of orange, yellow
Now added blues and pinks
Artificially aided, sitting in awe
An occasional deer sneaks up
The frogs and crickets sing
Way in the background
Out near the creek, an owl
Chimes in, a natural melody
Now our politicians move
To end this outdoor activity
A camaraderie of friends
Again, seeking to divide us
The more they try, the more
We push back in a group
To our elected leaders, Screw You!
Thru the blue smoke, on we go

D Everett Newell 6/30/2023

Bricks of Life

You come into this life
A baby held in your family's arms
Day by day you build your life
Brick by brick, slowly, surely
Every grade in school ascended
Every syllable you learn to speak
Challenges you pile up one by one
The building of you rises
Not a phoenix, but a peacock
Strutting around defiantly
At life's various stumbling blocks
Assimilating more at every event
Parties, outings, vacations, weddings
Even deaths continue our build
Onward we go for as long as we can
Till each person's train arrives at the station
Not always knowing when we are complete
Then on that day, the final ticket punched
We become a memory, vaporous to the ages
Hopefully thought on fondly by those remaining
Live every day fully, don't procrastinate
Day by day you build your life
Painstakingly Brick by brick!

D Everett Newell 10/20/2022

Brilliance

Having a great mind
Is overrated, why?
You have all those meaningful ideas
Stored in your brain
No room for the zany things
One does when not being smart
I'm a prime example of this phenomenon
There are absolutely no great ideas
Found within my cranium
I've proven this hypothesis daily
I've proven this over many years
I'm consistent in my thinking
Don't want to burn out
Before my time is up, pacing
Is my best method to longevity
So go on, I double dare you
To find one iota, one scintilla
Of proof of my Brilliance!

D Everett Newell 12/16/2021

Bucket List

We all have hopes and desires
Things we want to accomplish
Via school, work, families
Our so-called bucket lists
Mine is vast,
Mostly here in the confines of America
But as I age, physical prowess weaken
What I can do realistically shrinks
It is ok, we all make the cluttered beds
We lie upon, not always willingly
At times we incrementally do not notice
Till we realize the many changes
I've done, seen, and I've heard a lot
Traveled my fair share
Seeing concert after concert
I like the human condition, its stories
Always been intrigued
With history and traditions
But I know I'll never see The Alamo
Knowing now I'll never get to New Orleans
Nor will I visit Pearl Harbor
The OK Corral, Pacific Ocean and more
I won't fly, driving gets harder
Coupled with the expense of it all
Now I do what I can, promise I enjoy it
Always love everything I experience
All who I experience it with
But I have now a leaky rusted container
Listen to me, do it now while you can
Go after your Bucket List vigorously

D Everett Newell 12/9/2022

Bumping Uglies

Walking down our local street
Able and Jen marched hand in hand
Just happy to be alive
And enjoying the days together
What could go wrong
Well, for these two, almost everything
You see, Able was not always agreeable
Jen grew very frustrated
Loving Able, but needed much more
She wanted to always go left, he right
Day after day leading to fights
Both growing apart, bickering
Hurt feelings, now loathing
Dreading to be with one another
But habits hard to break
We go all in on bad arrangements
Either too scared to end them or too lazy
Finally it exploded, a huge blow up
Right there for all to see
Both turned to leave, but turned right into each other
Able's body swallowed Jen, fitting snugly
They now were the definition of bumping uglies

D Everett Newell 12/16/2021

Chariots

Vehicles of all shapes, colors
Sizes, two-door, four-door
Manual or automatic transmission
Two or four wheeled
My bastions of independence
First a two-tone blue '64 Olds
You were a beast, I loved you
Then I broke your heart
Traded you in for a '69 Pontiac
Around the same time, thrilling
Move into a 1971 Honda
Motorcycle, flashy brilliant red
Many, too many to mention
Followed for fifty years after
I look back fondly
At each of you, all
Giving me freedoms of
Being able to call my own
Shots, my own projector
Thank you always
To my life's chariots

D Everett Newell 1/7/2022

Cheers

Let's raise a glass
To a life of memories
In its honor
Let's raise a glass
To friends here and lost
In their honor
Let's raise a glass
To many battle scars acquired
In their honor
Let's raise a glass
To the hope of our tomorrows
In their honor
Let's raise a glass
To the brilliant night moon
In its honor
Let's raise a final glass
To the days renewal in brilliant sun
In its honor

D Everett Newell 11/5/2022

Clown and Silver Balls

Have you ever
Seen a clown with silver balls?
Have you ever
Watched him walking with red floppy shoes?
Have you ever
Seen him spritz others with water?
You see, he is there to make us laugh
Make us forget the moment
A clown's job is to evoke laughter
As they honk their horns
Juggle their many silver balls
Ride their "too small" bikes
Throwing buckets of rice on each other
Why I ask you,
Seriously, why?
Do clowns scare the hell out of us?
Have you ever
Seen a scary clown, with his silver balls?

D Everett Newell 11/30/2021

Commercial TV

I'm alarmed more and more
As more subliminal messages
Come across my television screen
Driving a complete assault
On the traditional family pyramid
I was raised to respect my elders
To love family elders completely
Cherishing their story and their life-lived
Now, I'm told over and over
Don't grow up to be my parents
This is insulting to me on so many levels
Praying I could ever be a measure
Of what they've been
Parental wisdom, their idioms
Learning tools that taught me
How to daily go about my business
With integrity, honesty, humanity
I find absolutely no humor
No need to be instructed
By actors, on how I should act
I'll trust in those that came before me
Rather than ever listening to commercial TV

D Everett Newell 1/13/2022

Confusion

The day breaks, after coffee I sit
Thoughts hit me in waves
Happy, sad, happy then sad again
For every good thought, a bad one comes in
I fight this balance in my life
Growing exhausted, bewildered, angry
Winter blues, coupled with illness and absence
Loneliness, worries, lack of sun
Conspiring against me, pushing me
To a dark side I want no part of
A struggle like no other
Weary, tired, isolated, hurt emotionally
Feeling awake, but drifting away
I'm just so perplexed, up then down
One of those mornings my life
Takes a trek, to confusion

D Everett Newell 12/28/2021

Some days we all struggle to resist the dark side, but we fight always

Consort

Jumping to a new sound
Balls bouncing are inbound

Skipping quickly over this mess
Slows me down in life's game of chess

Sliding, slipping, I start to fall
But not quite yet, I grab a wall

A mess of proportional size
Slowing my breath, then I sigh

Obstacle course is now my reality
Keeping composure, I exclaim cordially

Forgive me all for my clumsiness
Smiling, I laugh with complete politeness

Then on to my eventual day's work
Spending time with my peers, time to consort

D Everett Newell 2/2/2022

Corner of My Eye

Sitting just past the edge of spring
Clouds look ugly this morn
A storm possibly on schedule
Nature flexing its muscles again
Grey darkness floats overhead
Trees, naked, bend to its power
I hear birds squawking with news
No human now in my sight
All I assume, hunkered down
The change of our seasons
Always brings surprise, an unsure state
Having done this many, many times
Yet still waiting with anticipation
Some flowers already poking heads out
As the sky opens, blue peeks through
I start a new awakening, a renewal
A wanted yellow shard shines down
As I catch it in the corner of my eye

D Everett Newell 3/24/2022

Country Boy

Loved waking up,
Watching the sun
Come up over the rolling hills
Mist lifting as it's burned off
Our valley coming alive
More car traffic,
Here and there, people moving
Waking in this small town
Slowly, friendly, with a purpose
There was no locking of doors
All homes, businesses,
Cars left open
I remember the milkman
Driving slowly house to house,
Delivering the thirst quenching drinks
Newspapers from bicycles being thrown
Rider of not necessarily good aim
Then walking the two blocks to school
Everywhere trees, animals, nature
We co-existed together, mingling freely
People I remember were friendlier then
This new global world has ruined that
Often, I think and wish I could go back
For you see, I'm a simple guy
Like living in my era
Always at heart,
I remain just a country boy

D Everett Newell 1/28/2022

Cranky

I, as I'd want to do
Had a dream the night past last
Weird as they tend to be for me
Seeing myself as 18 again, one day
A day out of the many memories
Could not believe my good luck
Being that whirlwind of a day, I did it all
Suddenly as it started, it ended
Waking up frightful, unnerving me
So glad to know I was me
70-plus with all the wrinkles, and pains
You see when I realized how lucky I am
As much as I'd like to relive life
Never could I risk all that I have
The memories I've made
My family, kids, grandkids, great-grand kid
Friends I've known a lifetime
Losing all that, never acceptable
As my time draws down, I'm happy
My path was as it should have been
Had my fun, yeah the many heartaches
But saying to myself, I'm good
Living is complicated, mine not a masterpiece
Flawed as we all are time to time
I accept me as I am
Even the days I'm a bit dusty
A bit worn, used up
A bit cranky

D Everett Newell 2/17/2024

Crazy Side

Have you ever
Just felt crazy
Wanted to be wild
Unfettered dancing in the rain
The mood strikes me
Every now and then
Don't know why
I've never questioned it
A feeling strikes up the band
Of uncontrollable whimsy
That lies dormant inside
I become a volcano
Of nope… he should have not done that
To… I can't believe he just did that
Wish I could explain
No drugs or alcohol needed
Added charges never the case
Just intrinsic to me
Myself and I, as I sometimes
Walk on the crazy side

D Everett Newell 2/2/2022

Curiosity

You know how it is said
Curiosity gets the best of us
Or curiosity kills the cat
It's one of the human traits,
I respect the least
Even I fall to this worthlessness
See an ambulance next door
Necks and eyes strain to get the scoop
Car wreck on freeway
Traffic slows to see mangled flesh and metal
Breaking news on TV
We are glued to latest catastrophe
Maybe its makes us feel better
Seeing others at their worst moments
I can't explain, I wish I could
Maybe humans are just plan nosy
I try to stop, to be a better me
Sometimes I just can't
Wracked with guilt, yet
Being overcome with curiosity

D Everett Newell 6/03/2015

Darla Nightmare

Lying in bed, windows open
Getting comfortable in my spot
Cool air wafting over me
I snuggle into my single bed cover
This will be a great night to sleep
I can't quite relax, I fidget, roll
At some point, seemed like hours
Drifting off, at least that's what the clock said
When I glanced its way
Suddenly, I hear a loud noise, focusing
Loud short intermittent blaring sounds
Not ambulance, firetruck, or police
Different, alarming, riveting, unnerving
Sitting up in bed, then standing up
Wandering through our house to the living room window
Looking out, I hear a deep vibration
As if a tornado is baring down
Then I see bright sparkling light
Phosphorus orange, red, blues, falling near
A bounce and a boom between properties
Our two neighbors own, here I awaken
I have to go to the bathroom, but
I'm too afraid to move, after this Darla nightmare

D Everett Newell 5/3/2022

I Did

I sit here, still in disbelief
A week past, I sat
Where giants walked before me
Harpers Ferry, your beauty shined
At the Shenandoah and Potomac confluence
Gliding up and down your rises
Across your bridges, breathtakingly
Knowing I went where our fathers had
Jefferson and Washington stepped here
The great Appalachian Trail
Crossed your glorious rocky paths
Lewis and Clark used you
To forage a map and routes to the West
A great war laid at your doorstep
The radical abolitionist Brown
Came to terrorize and burn
Yes a just cause, a madman
Ignited a spark that changed us
As I reflect, put pen to paper
I'm overwhelmed at all the visions
My visit Took in,
So thankful I did

D Everett Newell 8/18/2022
Dedicated to My Rat Pack, you all know who you are, Thank you.

Different Experiences

Thought we were different
Thinking we are the only ones
But hold on, really
We weren't unique or special with
Our family's designed historic meals
The many traditions and quirks,
In reality shared by many others
The cloak of invisibility
Failed us, laughing now,
I realize how we were
So much more alike than different
To our neighbors around this world
Ones that ate boxes of pizza mix, or
Peanut butter and pickle sandwich
Maybe special fried dough dodgers
Pickled Beet eggs at Easter
Foods traditionalized
By many other iterations
Routinely eaten by we the populace
Secrets stolen, amended, shared
These are signs of societal glue
Showing more of the sameness
We share as a people,
Than a oneness
That in itself warms me
Makes me feel closer
To you all fellow men, and women
So, I'm grateful for all the years
Our interactions that
Provided my human canvas with
So many memorable colored experiences

D Everett Newell 10/3/2022

Different

People come in all sizes
Colors, religions, and more
I love people that are different
Makes my life, our world, interesting
Mundane it would be if all alike
Differences should be welcome
This sparks self-growth, an assimilation
We are all made up of many parts
Things we see, smell, touch incorporated
Not fitting as a square peg
Into that round hole, a badge of honor
Embrace the misfits, we of the weird
Don't be afraid of new experiences
They are a breath of the freshest air
In a world filled with hate
They bind us in humor, wonder, love
Questioning is OK, when done rightfully
We all like to be noticed, understood
Stand up hard for the downtrodden
Use fairness as binding tool
What I'm saying is – Welcome all
All who choose to be different
Coloring our world of many shades
That the sun shines down, and
As the moon illuminates brilliantly

D Everett Newell 2/25/2024

Dire Was Our Baby

This tale is one of the heart
And taking seed in the soul
Never mind his name
Bringing much joy to his family
This little guy was blessed
Despite the tragic prognosis
His Mom and Dad of many months
Months of hell, for you see
This was not an ordinary baby
Diagnosed with a birth defect
So horrific 90% do not survive
But through this perilous journey
Be damned the statistics
God intervened and the tide shifted
Outcome now is to live his life
A miracle that proved
Hope is never to be abandoned
In the most incredible storms
We pray, we march on
And then pray more, believing
That good is intrinsic
It will win out
As in this case and many more
Ignore when you hear
Dire now is not our Baby

D Everett Newell 11/28/2022

Disco Duck

Once upon a time
In the hamlet of Olcott NY
To a bar of our choice
A legend was hatched
With a precession of vehicles
Lead by a car with one eye
Ready to celebrate a birthday
Not every day you turn twenty-one
Friends in tow, fun to be had
Drinks of every type lined up
Then down the hatches of revelers
Coin after coin
Into our mechanical band
And it played and played
Songs of the day,
We danced and drank away
Then a bright idea
Let's take my moves to the tabletop
Up I went, as the sound
Loudly, proudly, burst out
Disco…Disco Duck…
Then it happened
As my stage started to break
A waitress ended the show
Unplugging the Juke Box in use
Demanding I come down
But not before she was coerced
Into singing one last verse

D Everett Newell 2/7/2022

Dedicate to my Buddy Dave Hickey who witnessed the night's atrocities
Now everyone sing, "Disco, Disco Duck"

Do Guns Kill

The question for all of us
Do guns kill
A basic, very basic idea
Burning the societal minds
Are firearms responsible
For murder in all our cities
Maybe, just maybe
We have become desensitized
To human suffering and death
I ask why for most of our history
This problem was not as evident
In my day, friends brought
Weapons to school for rifle club
People kill people, many ways
Mental health is responsible
Let's start by identifying
The root cause of a horrific era
We can fix it
I ask again, do you
Believe an intrinsic object
Can kill? So
Do guns kill?

D Everett Newell 1/8/2022

Downsizing Hurts My Heart

We all collect too much stuff
Most of us do, I think
Preparing for our next garage sale
Sorting through past histories
Old memorable items from relatives
Ones that have passed on
Of course, saving some
Impossible to save all
Now we divide, grade, price
Things that meant the world
To our loved ones, seems cold
As we go about our business
A two-headed monster
At my own demise, coming
Probably sooner than I'd like
Someone will sit around tables
Processing our lives
I'd expect them to do just that
Painful activity we leave
To our future, loved family
Downsizing hurts my heart.

D Everett Newell 5/4/2022

Dull Me

In heaven,
Am I stripped
Of my earthly possessions
Personality void of pain
Mobility issues gone,
Walking once more
Will I be an old man?
A young man,
Still awkward, crude?
Or will life's polishings
Go with me? I ponder,
These ideas a lot, I wonder
I question, do any of you?
Do score cards exist? I asked
My pastor cousin, how I get
Extra credits, I'd love to have
A room with a view, hot tub
One floor plan, all the dogs
I have ever known,
Of course, in heaven, you know
They would not poop, in fact
Maybe none of us would
Hope I don't change a lot
After I get there, really
No need for a dull me

D Everett Newell 2/17/2022

Dying Bugs Me

Dying really frosts my ass
I mean it will piss me off
My whole life, wondering
Leaving me perplexed
That every conduit, idea, experience
I've ever had
Goes away with my demise
Haunting me,
I have so much to tell
My mind has always worked to share
Really can't believe it will be all gone
As I take that last breath
Like turning the light off at night
Just black, void
I feel a part of all I ever touched
They will disappear also
My thoughts, experience, good and bad
Like a rested Wikipedia
Where does it all go?
Yeah, dying will bug me

D Everett Newell 2/3/2022

Elders

The most value we have
Are housed
Inside the minds and souls
Of each family's crusty warriors
In each of our houses
Resides our loving elders,
Waiting to be called
We should all leap
Or jump at the chance
To sit around them
In a circle of love and listen
As long and as far
As they can remember
Their stories, histories,
Demand to be shared
Then passed down
By each of us
Much like the Native Americans
Passed down their languages
To new layers of generations
Not doing this, is criminal
Ending in a massive loss
Trust me what we'd hear
Is pure silver and gold
Worth more than any tangible item
Honoring them, by listening
Letting them know how important
They are to our lives
Is the greatest gift we can give

I beseech you, and call on you
To take that time and do it
I guarantee you'll never be sorry
I know all sides benefit
When time is spent with our elders

D Everett Newell 11/22/2021

Dedicated to all my Great Grand Parents, Grand Parents & Parents, who have given me so much!!!!!!!!

Elixir of Life

The seed is dropped
Then covered in soil
Lying dormant till life comes
Sprouting then stretching
Reaching for the sunlight
Drinking the clear sparkling morning dew
Growing and a beauty starts to emerge
A flower dainty colorful but strong
A strength inherent to what it is
What it shows us, its survival
Lights a path for our species
As we also grow steadily
From a seedling to a being
We sprout and stretch
Reaching for sunlight, our unique life
A quest like no other
Individual to each as we assimilate
Souls grow, hearts beat
Brains function in so many ways
This elixir of life runs through all
Everything on our shared planet
Lives to its own journey

D Everett Newell 3/1/2024

Emotions

My long-loved Team
Lost in a big game again
When you hear a friend
Clings to life, a battle
Not likely to win
I won a big gamble
Sports betting the last week
The frigid air nips at my nose
But the brilliant sun
Glaring off the pure white snow
Warms my heart, bringing smiles
The ups and downs of life's rollercoaster
Seeing news, the virus still kills
Russian troops set to invade
The powerful talking down to the powerless
Looking for kindness daily
Seeing it in the many corners of life
Wow, just read another variant of Covid
Now in this once great country
Where or when will it ever end
It would be easy to give up
But I won't, I'll play out my hand
My charter to fight till I'm called home
The ups and downs of life's rollercoaster
Emotions are a perpetual see-saw

D Everett Newell 1/24/2022

Empathy

All we need from each other
Is to understand
The paths we each walk
Don't criticize right away
Take that step back,
Count to three
Most of us act on our life
Through experiences and interaction
Assimilated over time, rest easy
Just give that slight shadow
That allow glimmers
Of light's rays, giving hope
Erasing the boundaries and barriers
That separate us as one people
Building friendships and bonds
Are our greatest testament
The glue that will
Absolutely hold our society together
This takes practice, but exercise
Those muscles of mind and soul
Adding more empathy
In all we do!

D Everett Newell 2/3/2022

Evolved

When young, being headstrong confident,
Outgoing and quite liberal
Bell Bottoms, Long Hair, Platform shoes
Many floral purple, pink shirts
Blue jeans and my Army Jacket
Passionate about my world views
Hated all senseless wars, violence
Our music during that time, a voice
Protested establishment, the Man
Challenged and question all paradigms
Got married, had two kids
Gave up pieces of me
As more responsibility laid at my feet
My Drinking, carousing, slowed down
Sold my motorcycle and my canoe
Vestiges of an Era now in change
The wild child in me had diminished
I suppose that will never entirely die
Maturing through the years, family, work
Became my focus, my drive
Willingly surrendering all else
Embracing the trappings that joined
Buying a house, acquiring stuff
As most of us, slowly incrementally
Selling out a little as time passed
Kids now have kids of their own
On my second marriage, I'm different
What is important is how I'm different

I'm not radical or liberal,
I seem more than anything numb
That fire went out years ago
As is with most middle class
Working, living paycheck to paycheck
As I look in the mirror these days, I see
I'm not far-right or far-left
I'm just right of center
My belief, most of us are
It's been the awakening of me
Knowing security, safety, freedom
The bedrocks of our society
Pillars of our forefathers,
For our nation to succeed,
These must endure
Thru the trials
The tribulations of a life lived
A subtle transformation of a boy to man
My own metamorphosis, I evolved

D Everett Newell 4/19/2022

Exercise That Mind

I was not born
To be an old man
Thinking on it brings tears
How did I get here
Assured it was not on purpose
Kicking and screaming the whole way
Begrudgingly and slowly the years passed
Looking now in the mirror
I don't recognize the view
No hair, fatter face, wow
Yet inside, inside the young soul
Remains steadfast, agile, ready
Thinking I could still be me
Taking a first step, realizing
Nope, the mechanics are worn and rusty
How now can I merge the two me's
Not possible to do so
Compromise is the answer, so be it
Even though I detest caving in
I must, adapting to a new version
Not mobile, still mentally flexible
I'll continue to exercise that muscle

D Everett Newell 11/24/2022

Fairy Tale

I like fairy tales
Seeing life much like one
My home is my castle
So then, my wife is a Queen
All of it, runs through her
Our family, well taken care of
In her very capable hands
Part mechanic, plumber
Cook, housekeeper working out
Loving me and our girls
I ask to slow down, take it easier
Relax some, enjoy your fruits
As we grow older, things change
Takes longer to do everything
But that always is OK
What is important is we are both here
I can't imagine life without
Can't imagine our castle without
Its Queen, completing my fairy tale

D Everett Newell 3/30/2022

To Kathy, my all, my everything!

Fears

All I ever wanted to be
  I allowed fears to stop me
A pro baseball player
  I allowed fears to stop me
Going parachuting with my buddy
  I allowed fears to stop me
Taking supervisory position, then stepped down
  I allowed fears to stop me
Now as I write and speak
  I always fight fears from stopping me
Fears, Fears, Fears
  Don't allow them
    To STOP YOU!

D Everett Newell 12/02/2021

Five W's

What happened
To us as a society
What day
Did common decency die
Who decided
Crime would win
Who decided
We'd discard our homeless
When then
Will we get back to us
When will
We regain the nuclear home
Why do
Our leaders not lead
Why is hate
Fostered over everything
Where will I
Go to find peace
Where can I
Live without fear

D Everett Newell 1/31/2022

Flavors of Christmas

As the fireplace crackles
The tastes and flavors arise
As Christ would one day do
Christmas is once more
As we celebrate his day
The day he was born
Eggnog is poured into festive mugs
Hot coco is being warmed on the stovetop
Marshmallows lay in wait, to jump in
Flour is poured, stirred amid eggs and sugar
Formed into many seasonal shapes
Candy canes and fudge await
The constant march to our mouths
Many family dishes being prepared
As dishes, silverware clash and clink
Candles are lit, trees are ablaze
In bright lights of many hues
And the music, spiritual, happy
Heartwarming traditional music
This is the pallet that makes up
All our flavors of Christmas

D Everett Newell 12/1/2021

Fridays

Here I sit, upon a precipice
On to a weekend soon enjoined
What wonders shall I enjoy
As hours click by slowly
Remembering the long days worked
In my life as if yesterday
The weeks came
They mundanely passed
Seven-day schedules,
Completely using me up
Missing many family celebrated events
And numerous holidays
Earning the green to feed and house
Supporting my family
As was the expected
Now retired, my calendar empty,
I'm ready to party but
Guess what,
Time marches still forward
To my surprise, still grudgingly
Vacant vacuums of sitting alone
It would seem everyone else,
Now busy,
A catch-22 to be sure
Looking to my Saturday and Sundays
Natural breaks in the boring, yet
There are no lines of demarcation
All blended into one long period
So here I sit upon that precipice
On to a weekend, in all probability lost again

D Everett Newell 9/23/2022

Funny how life is, for a huge part, you're too busy to enjoy it, then when you can it might be too late

Fruit Belt

Growing up in Western New York
I've been lucky, one of the richest
In produce in the world
Starting in early June
Strawberry season opens with a bang
Shortcake and ice cream galore
As that ends, cherries take their bow
Going to the many fruit markets
Gathering our weekly shares
White and dark cherries are
All the rage, taking the stage
Then as it dies down, peaches
Plums, nectarines, pears
Burst upon us, demanding attention
That takes us to August
And late that month, Ginger Gold
Rings in the apple season
Living here in the summer
A glorious feast, nature's bounty
Putting on weight, needing to let out
My wonderful fruit belt

D Everett Newell 12/15/2021

Gettysburg

I feel you calling me
I hear you calling me

Upon my first visit
60 long years ago
I knew I belonged to you

I feel you calling me
I hear you calling me

In your presence I feel calm
I am centered like nowhere else
Knowing I am home once again

I feel you calling me
I hear you calling me

Loving to show others about you
A mystical place like no other
Memories flood my senses completely

I feel you calling me
I hear you calling me

There will come a time
I'll be back for good
Perpetually a part of you

I feel you hugging me
I'll hear you whisper my name

D Everett Newell 3/3/2024

Glass Houses

"Let thee, not cast
The first rock"
Yet we see a lot
Of that in our world
Since the birth of Social Media
Many cowards sit behind
Glass cased monitors
Saying any rude thing
They write, things never
Would be stated in person,
Looking face-to-face
What has happened to us
Culturally we should evolve
Instead, collectively
Standing in sewers knees deep
So easy to argue,
Throw negative comments
While we are alone
Isolated, change please
Try saying constructive ideas
Try being a change agent
Try complimenting
Versus tearing down
Simply said, "Do not cast
The first rock,
Understand we all
Live in glass houses!"

D Everett Newell 2/2/2022

Good Morning All

Cold house as I walk through
Breezy you may say
Hearing the wind whip outside
Brings various cringes as I move
Funny how our imagination,
 Makes things worse
Reality usually,
Is less than perceived
As is most of our lives
Snow-capped grass,
 Fighting to survive
Envision, snow with green measles
Floors as I walk upon them
 Feel like glassy ice
Numbness takes over
Stooping over, slowly pulling on my slippers
Enjoining a dull ache
Joints start throbbing together
In that painful chorus
One I hate, but have
 Become accustomed to
Envelopes me, reaching for
Many types of pain meds that mask
I put on a hat and slowly finish dressing
I heard that keeps heat in
Things are better now
Top, bottom covered, now
To slowly get dressed
Good Morning All

D Everett Newell 3/29/2022

Good Ole Days

Well, we always wish
For the good old days
Our memories are such
We mostly remember the good
The bad we stuff, stored
In the file cabinets
At the very back of our brains
In reality,
It's nature's coping mechanism
Keeping us sane
Keeping us attached,
In the game
As we age, wear down, wear out
Pains, pills creep in
All becoming constant companions
I spend a lot of my time
Sitting in reflection
Of years past
Still I feel the laughter,
All the happy tears
And yes,
I dread
The unknown of tomorrows
Uncertainties of the life
We know await
But fear of this can't stop us
Must always remember
Those days as
Fright rears its ugly head

Today is always
Our best day
Spend it fully and wisely
Tomorrow is unknown
Yesterday was
and forever will be
The Good Old Days

D Everett Newell 1/4/2022

Great Puzzle of Humanity

How do we fit into this world
Something I ponder on
I believe all of us
Have uneven, ragged edges
We compromise, change
In small degrees, not ever
Completely compromising
But will conform gradually
Life is about stealing
We take a little of this
Then a little of that
Assimilating from various
Pieces of all we encountered
The great thing is we are all different
None of us the same
Yet all similar in subtle ways
A glorious thing in the end
Making this,
A great puzzle of humanity

D Everett Newell 2/3/2022

Greed and Hate

This sharp double-bladed weapon
One like Damocles' sword
We are exposed daily
And assimilate, as much as we try not
Bad virtues, a ruination of man
Exposed to the bone
In every waking walk of life
No one can completely, truly
Escape the wrath shown continually
Yet we have to resist and reset
A war against modern-day twins
Like the Apollo and Artemis
Of Greek mythology, our twins
Live to deceive and divide us
Let us rise, resist, and conquer
Greed and hate, till they
Are vanquished from this earth

D Everett Newell 6/15/202

Haloes

Angels wear haloes
My mind's eye perception
From what I've always been told
By my side when needed
I only need to call
God's warriors will charge
A shield against darkness
Do they also reside inside
The vastness of my head, within
The darkest crevices, where evil
My largest worries manifest
They must, right,
They help silently
Daily survive this
Sometimes-bleak world
I appreciate all their help
Wondering if they dress like us
Pants, dresses, shorts, etc.
When they look in heaven's mirrors
Do they look like us
In my mind they always light up
Glowing, effervescence brightly
And yes, for a hat,
Their beautiful adornment
Shining, radiant haloes

D Everett Newell 2/1/2022

Happenstance

I was just out walking
On a bright sunny day
Funny, it was almost perfect
Birds chirping, squirrels scurrying
Clouds casting shadows in their passing
My, my, what do we have here?
You walked into my peripheral vision
Seeing enough of you, I turned my head
Wow, I thought, what a lovely creature
See, I believe love is just that
No planning, a chemical release
Pheromones, captivating, a strong response
How many of us were immediately struck
By a random person near us
Without notice, no planning, instant
Now, this is not seed for a
Long time relationship, but
Staying with us forever, the one
Who beckoned to us
Knocked us off our proverbial feet
All because of chance and happenstance

D Everett Newell 1/27/2022

Hate

Teardrops shed again
How can I address demons
Nothing I can say helps
Heal despair, loss, anger
I know it has to stop
Only we can change things
Don't look to politics to heal
They'll fail us miserably
Like ripples in a calm lake
Hugging each with our hearts
Will drive tsunamis of love
Be kind to one another
Support, encourage as much as possible
Be positive change agents
Turn negative TV news off
Let's hand in hand build
A world we can be proud of
In starts with each of us
Only we can stop the hate

D Everett Newell 5/25/2022

He Sleighs It

Santa Claus is coming,
I've been told
Love it when he stops by
Bringing merriment when he does
Hearing hoofbeats upon rooftops
Coming down a chimney hard
One that magically appears
Leaving the usual cookies, milk
And carrots – yep, can't forget those
A jolly laugh and rotund belly
We could be brothers
From another mother
It's a two-fold holiday
One of Christ our Savior
And this fat old man
You know what— it works!
Religion and magic, hard to beat
Believe in both if you can
Keeping us all young at heart
And hopefully pure of soul
I love Christmas. I love Christ
I love Santa. He sleighs it

D Everett Newell 12/8/2022

Headstone

When I'm gone, nothing will mark me
Well, at least not a plot of ground
Nor a stone monument to my life
What I'm leaving behind is me
My memories with all I love
Friends, family,
And anyone who crossed my path
In a life verociously lived
My words will mark what and who I was
How I thought, my travels
Tall tales, dreams,
My many hopes, disappointments
Pictures taken of us,
Will help boost all
To everyone who knew me
I will live forever, I hope
Within your minds, memories
I will be passed down as such
Like Native American speech
From Generation to Generation
Smile when my name comes up
Laugh a bit, know it's my wish
Promising you, I will not have
A gravesite to visit,
Mine belongs to the winds
As they move me
Across my favorite places
Dust by dust, amiably moved
That will be my forever headstone

D Everett Newell 3/25/2022

I'm convinced that our human form is just a capsule and once
Our Spirit is gone, so is our essence

Heaven Shared

So, what is your vision
Or version of heaven
Do we all get our own slice
Inside a plastic bubble
Much like a Broadway play
With shared family and friends
Characters in a grand display
Of all that was good in living
What age do we exist
Hope we are free of illness
Or the multiples of stress
Earth journeys give us
Maybe we are all
On the same plane
But how is it all managed
Divorced, do you then have two spouses
All of it makes we wonder, ponder
Pause, reflect,
All of it amusing then
Scares me, freezes me as I don't
Do the unexpected with grace
So I ask, do you ever wonder
About your Heaven shared

D Everett Newell 10/18/2022

Heaven

What is yours
Is there any way
To measure time
If so, in what appearance
Are we baby, child, youth, adult
Or worn and ragged
All of us have different visions
Do we immediately see all lost
Like layers of a cake
Or skins of an onion
Cutting through each decade
I can wait to find out
Being in no real rush
Though it would be easier
If I knew what to expect
Then planning better
Knowing what I should pack
How is the weather, hot, cold, neither
Having many many questions
They rear up each time
I lose someone dear to me
And the many dear to family
Thinking I'll see them again
But thinking I need to be better
To get to my version of heaven

D Everett Newell 1/29/2022

High on the Mountains

High on the mountains
Birds fly high, the glorious clouds
The deer run in valleys
Where the rivers flow
Trees growing green
Tall, very proud, rooted firmly
It's a honor to view all
From the highest perch
Nothing knows I'm there
All the better, as there
Are no interruptions below
To this vast moving show
Dreaming, feeling, flying
Emotions all joined, truly
As the Bible states, honestly
Yes, my cup runneth over
High on the mountains

D Everett Newell 1/8/2022

Hotdog

Being a kid from western Pennsylvania
To an adult living in western New York
We take our foods very seriously
Like the infamous hotdog
Not really a healthy treat
Nonetheless one we like to eat
Now listen up as I tell you
Our hotdogs come fully dressed
Seated in a steamed footlong bun
The grilled sausage or fried bologna
Is placed like royalty on a throne
Toppings are serious, placed with
Great responsibility one upon another
Building this insane delicacy
A long bead of yellow mustard
Followed by a hot meat sauce
Throwing on a lot of minced onions
Finally joining the party, sweet pickle relish
Now all that is left is up to you
Me, I wolf this puppy down
This work of art, my very own
Western Pennsylvania's hotdog

D Everett Newell 10/28/2022

Dedicated to Reid's & Nicks Hotdogs in DuBois PA, which now belong to the dust bins of history!

Hours Wasted

Going to bed at night
Getting up in the morning
Hours wasted as life shortens
Seems that rotation on speed-dial
Wish I could figure out
Ways to rest my sore achy bones
I really don't ever sleep deep
Nights are left to rolling around
Five minutes here, then over there
When I do drift off, encountered
Are the many fragments of dreams
One could never imagine
To be comfortable again, my wish
Yet no genie in a bottle to help
Not ready to concede or give up
Fighting through each night
Only to restart on a short day
Going to bed at night
Getting up in the morning
Hours wasted as life shortens
Hours wasted, hours wasted

D Everett Newell 10/30/2022

Hummingbird

Brown oval dirt track
A dust bowl of my youth
The roar of gas-powered engines
Disappearing through a hay bale
Into the surrounding night
Rolling possibly down
That steep hill
Before the inglorious quick stop
Round and round they ran
Colors of cars
Speeding, blurred in my front
Metal gladiators compete at night
Multi-shaped,
So many various colored chariots
Excitement is felt,
Electric and unbridled
This is not scripted, furious they go
Then a finish
Where a Champion crowned!
Another night in the quiet country
When for a few hours, a hell let loose
Thank you for my lifelong memory
Near my boyhood home, Falls Creek PA
The forever known — Hummingbird

D Everett Newell 9/14/2022

I'll never forget my simpler happier youth, The People & Hills of PA, I'm forever your Son!

I love Gettysburg

Making Me Happy
Traveling over hill then dale
Route 15 South, my mood brightens
Making me happy
As we close in, the signs start
Gettysburg, next five exits
Making me happy
Now passing cannons, monuments
Tablets that tell of its history
Making me happy
All my friends in tow, getting to hotel
The Gettysburg Best Western
Making me happy
We are sleeping on part of the battlefield
The soldiers' cemetery across the street
Making me happy
Staying on Steinwehr Ave, a conduit
To everything we love
Making me happy
Down this street, the Dobbin House
Or Appalachian Brewhouse
Making me happy
We are a short drive away
From Little Round Top and Culps Hill
Making me happy
Walking into town, to the Square
All businesses and souvenirs a plenty
Making me happy
Bus tours, ghost tours or by carriage

Many more ways to explore
Making me happy
Spent so many hours and days
With my beloved family and friends
Always have made me happy

D Everett Newell 12/8/2022

I Promise

No one loves me
As much as I do
Promise you, this is true

My poems are works of genius
I have on paper my proof
It's a mantle of pride

No one loves me
As much as I do
Promise you, this is true

The confidence you need
To share your written thought
Is unmeasurable

No one love me
As much as I do
Promise you, this is true

D Everett Newell 3/11/2022

Written for Kathy V. Newell, my wife

I Said

I said, I'd like a milkshake
You said, will see
I said, love a fresh-baked pie
You said, will see
I said, maybe Sunday good day for ham
You said, will see
I said, let's win huge wealth
You said, will see
I said, I want to be with you forever
You said, will see
I said, guess I have a lot of wants
You said, I see
I said, you see or will see
What will be, will be

D Everett Newell 3/29/2022

I See More Clearly

Remembering all my time spent
With a man of men
Lumberjack, hunter, fisher
A great man, humble strength
He, being in his ninth decade
Spent time with me in my first
One of life's greatest treasures
My memories being there
Smelling his pipe smoke, sweet
Sitting under a huge old oak
Listening to Pirate's baseball
The day he gave me a book
Loaded with animals of all kind
In it he wrote,
"I want this young boy to have my book"
I still have it Great Granddad
Till, I join you in heaven
If I happen to be that lucky
Thank you for the foundation
You helped set, because of you
Always I see more clearly

D Everett Newell 2/2/2022

Dedicated to Great Grand Father Berkey

I Walk the Valley

I walk the valley
Above life moves at will
Blue skies, pocked
With many puffy white clouds
Noise abounds, branches move
The wind exercises them up then down
Birds flying, chirping away
Wolves howl, elk in rut
Dancing their dominate dance
Life is beautiful, taking it in
I'm sure all smile
Experiencing nature unbridled
God's pallet is boundaryless
A gift every day
All we need do, is look
Simple for us to just enjoy
Don't question, take it as it is
Sights and sounds that calm
Yea! I walk the valley
Breathtaking, every vibrant step
So thankful I can

D Everett Newell 1/31/2022

Idiotic or Iconic

The idea of Bigfoot
    Idiotic or Iconic
The idea of the Weiner Mobile
    Idiotic or Iconic
The idea of Punxy Phil the Groundhog
    Idiotic or Iconic
The idea of Mothman
    Idiotic or Iconic
The idea of Aliens among us
    Idiotic or Iconic
The idea of Leprechauns and Pots of Gold
    Idiotic or Iconic
The idea of the Paranormal
    Idiotic or Iconic
The idea of Good Luck Four Leaf Clovers
    Idiotic or Iconic
I have so many more questions
    Not enough answers

D Everett Newell 3/3/2024

If I could

If I could
I would end Covid, getting our lives back
If I could
I would end the senseless acts of violence
If I could
I'd make our economy prosperous for all
If I could
I'd invent glasses, through which we all see the sameness in each of us, not the differences
If I could
I'd make laughter and entertainment a standard, not an option
If I could
I'd end all wars with all people
People at their base are mostly good, the governments get in the way
If I could
I'd fix my Mom's broke brain
If I could
I'd hear my Dad's voice, and get his advice again

D Everett Newell 12/16/2021

I'll See You Again

Through the tears sometimes
We get rainbows
Those are the remnants
Of lives shared, being such
Memories well earned
Lucky to orbit this earth
Together at times
Enjoying the ups, being there
To support for the lows
At the time we don't think
About the end, the 'life ends' part
Surely in the back of each of our
Craniums, we know life's finality
Living goes on, has to
Memories never ever cease
God Bless You My Friend
Have a safe trip
I'll see you again

D Everett Newell 1/30/2022

I'm 17

Yes, I'm 17, and I have a passion
It burns red hot within me
I understand well, Think I know
The world is bigger than this valley
One that I was born to, raised in
Nothing greater than fighting
For home, country, and family
And God, it's my birthright
I hold both very tight to my chest
Yes, I must do what I must
My family, being a family of God
After much thought and convincing
Getting parents to consent
After much back and forth
I'm allowed to Volunteer
Joining the Army for the backend
Of a great War, World War II
Going through basic training
Flying to Europe, with others my age
Seeing and experiencing
Like I've never, before
Assigned to a bombers flight crew
Now part of the Buzz Job
My newest family unit
In the thick of it now
Bombing over Nazi controlled Europe
Horrendous deadly daily fighting
Seeing men, I trained with
New buddies die by the plane load

Exploding into fiery heaps
Angers wells up into tears
Knowing many more dying on the ground
My consciousness burns inside
Tears at my every fiber, being a Godly man
Not sleeping I pray nightly,
That I would be spared
Longing to be in the valley again
I suddenly feel like an old man
Looking in a mirror, I'm shocked
Dismayed to still see
A boy of seventeen looking back at me

D Everett Newell 12/02/2021
Dedicated to the best man I've ever known, John Everett Newell Jr.
Or My DAD!

I'm No Dope

Love is deep, it is true
Pulls me up, when I'm blue
Attached to you, as a string on soap
Proves to you it's real, I'm no dope
With heartfelt feelings, I look deep within
True and straight cupid's arrow,
Demanded it be let in
Undeniable, love at first sight
No sense in fighting it,
Recognizing I do what's right
Love is deep, it is true
Pulls me up, when I'm blue
Forever attached to you, as a string on soap
Proves forevermore, I'm no dope

D Everett Newell 12/1/2021

Journeys

We all have our private walks
Could be health's walls to climb
Losses pile up along our roads
Steadfast we keep heads down
Treading step after step, inch to mile
Onward we trek, can't stop
If we do, our legs become statues
Our hearts freeze over
Our brains become less
With each lost passing moment
At birth we start our trip
Continued until our heart has that final memorial
What happens in-between is
Left undefined, we color in those lines
Through our efforts to live
Each individual is unique
No two alike, choices made
Define who we are, how we end up
And how we enjoin our survived
Distinct, well-lived journeys

D Everett Newell 6/16/2022

Key

What is a key
Used to tune a song
Maybe that important person
Does it unlock doors?
A metallic object on its ring
Yes, all of the above
Helps us lead our lives
Opens doors to mind and soul
As well as wooden barricades
It's important to we
Who use them
Some say an aide to winning
Using these appropriately
And timely, recognizing
Each, and their importance
Certainly, is Key!

D Everett Newell 12/14/2021

Let Me Be

Pondering, this thought,
As it rushed at me
Hey mister, man with wealth
Have I got a plan
One you can't resist
You need a tax shelter
A business, you can
Count on, to go belly up
One that will lose money
Dollars you can write it off
I'm your man, I am,
I am a proven failure, honest
Pick any enterprise, let me
Weave my magic
You can trust in me
What is good, I'll make bad
I'm not good really at anything
At anything - well that makes money
Trust in what I tell you
It is detailed and documented
Having a long nonproductive
Track record
So I ask, no I beg
Let me be, your plan

D Everett Newell 12/03/2021

Let's Kill

Let's kill hate, indifference
Let's kill harmful cold words
Let's kill horrible actions
Let's kill each other with kindness
Let's kill, kill, kill
All the inhumanity to all
Stop the wars fought over nothing
Let's let all live as they are
Enjoy our many differences
Love, compassion makes us stronger
So please, each of us is a start
Together every hour of every day
Let's kill hate, indifference
Let's kill harmful cold words
Let's kill horrible actions
Let's kill all that kills our humanity

D Everett Newell 1/8/2022

Join in joining instead of finding ways to divide

Life is Fleeting

Life is fleeting
As you use it up
Squeeze it for all you can get
Tomorrow is not promised
Hold a measure of love to all
As much as possible
Be that positive force
Leave a memory of you
That is fondly remembered
Nothing matters more or
Is more cherished
Than sharing love, compassion
A fueled passion in living
Strive to be the one
For everyone and all
People are drawn to kindness
Be a magnet for them
Get as much as you can
Out of each waking moment
Life is fleeting
As you use it up
Squeeze it for all you can get
Did I make it very clear?
Life is Fleeting

D Everett Newell 1/24/2022

Lineage

Just like our family lineage,
Poetry found its way through time.
From Grandma Berkey,
To Cousin Dennis.
Now that blessing became mine.

Just like our family,
Our poems contain love.
Telling stories, solving life lessons,
And thanking the good Lord above.

When the time comes to return home,
Our words will remain like stone.
Passed on to our future generations,
Reminding them they will never be alone.

Zach "Noodles" Newell

Lonely Clown

Like a lonely clown
Always running around
Sad in their collective humor
What lies behind those painted faces

Lonely clown, why the frown
Is your life upside down
Fraught like all of us
Worries, life's everyday hassles
Wear out nerves, hurt the heart

Lonely clown, why the frown
Is your life upside down
Want to reach in
Where you reach out

Know we have an empathy
For you my friend
Looking for compassion
The passions need to thrive

Always note, no need
To continually live
Like a lonely clown
Always running around

D Everett Newell 12/02/2021

Lost

Do you ever feel lost
Like you don't belong
A piece of jigsaw puzzle
Dumped on the wrong board
Just change your perspective
Make a call, do something stupid
Fun, different, break a log jam
The many problems of this world
Can at times make skin crawl
Stress can drive us over the brink
Most of us have hours or days
We stumble around in a fog
It is normal, trust me, we all share
Don't let it disrupt you, get on track
Look to your long-time plans
Only a paradigm shift steadfast
A new view will set you free
Shrug it off, move on,
you have no choice
No need to forever feel empty
Out of gas, stuck or Lost!

D Everett Newell 7/23/2022

To everyone overwhelmed in the fast paced world we find ourselves!
Love you All!

Slip Away

In a lifespan of 69 years
How many minutes, hours, days
Have I fretted away
Idle thoughts to no purpose
Mortgaging my life without notice
My wish would lie unfulfilled
To cash in the thrown away for now
Spending more time with those
People, events, that really mattered
In the end, I'll shed a tear
Maybe many, as even now
A salty liquid runs down my cheek
Lesson of life seldom learned
Until it's too late, I urge all
Don't let the sands of your hourglass
Slip away, without spending them begrudgingly

D Everett Newell 2/11/2023

Lyrical Energy

The music starts and I perk up
Playing over and over
In reality and within my mind
Hearing the instrumental arrangements
A cacophony of vocal melody
Building a crescendo of melted sound
I need, no I have to hear
The words, the poetry, the message
Read the liner notes as I listen
Again and again, I play it
Messages being sent,
I want to understand
All of this makes music complete
The best to dance to, smile to
Changing my mode, setting forth
Memories from my yesterday
Wakes me up, changes me
Love this lyrical energy

D Everett Newell 1/31/2022

Maddox

You are the newest to land
Becoming a beautiful add
To this family's historic weave
My Great-grandson, so loved
Sixth in our Everett lineage line
Possessing the brightest blue eyes
Strong loud lungs, active now
Only 3 months old, but I see your destiny
Buddy, you're made of strong fiber
Stand tall, proud, it's your birthright
I may not be with you on this earth
For long of your fantastic voyage
Doubt I'll not those weird lettering
Always look to the stars
There I'll be shining back with support
I love you so much already
I'm so proud not again weird lettering
Enjoy the moments of your life
As they come fleeting and fast
Hold on to your family, nothing
And I mean nothing, is more of value
Be true to your inner soul
Trust your gut, it will lead soundly
Treat all people with respect
And prepare to walk away from those
Who do not reciprocate back
You are our newest treasure

It's time to take on
Our family mantle, carry it proudly
I pray peace, love, humility, health
Will always be by your side
We are so lucky you are ours!
Maddox Everett Staats

D Everett Newell 5/8/2024
Dedicated to Maddox Everett Staats, our 6th Everett

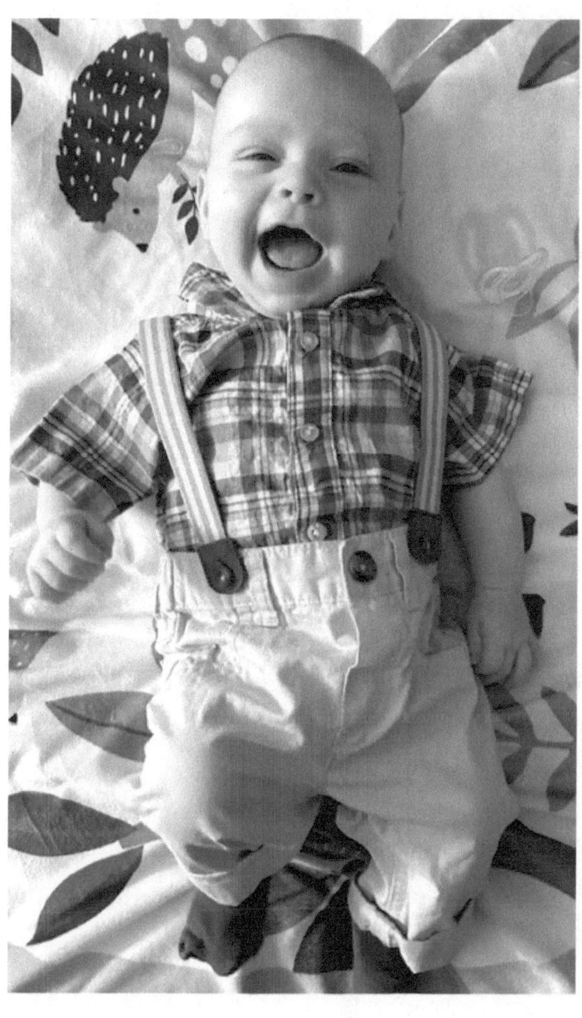

Memories, Both Good and Bad

Memories, both good and bad
They hold us up when sad
Can bring us down when glad
One thing steadfast and true
Weapons like these help you
Life is ours to experience
Adventures to retell at times of rest
Sometimes they cut deep to the quick
Other times just a minor wound, a prick
Adding up my toll in the end
Won't bring pots of gold to spend
Sorting things out will help me
To realize my path worn that all see
In summation, I do declare
Always take the time, be aware
Note to self: memories, our soul's sword
Yet all accomplished is our reward
Memories are both good and bad
Holding us up when sad
Bringing us down when glad

D Everett Newell 11/11/2022

Miracle

When people we care about
Close to us, ones we love
Are caught in troubled waters
We offer a prayer or prayers
We collectively keep them in thought
But in those dire times
We feel so helpless
Having not enough tools
In our many tool belts
Seems our words are matchsticks
Against the huge boulders of illness
Onward we go incrementally, day by day
Watching, hoping for progress
Looking to our Gods for help
Sometimes it's all for naught
Disheartening knives through our hearts
Yet on occasion, things line up
Not to be explained by we mortals
Then the skies lighten, and it happens
A miracle, so thankful they do!

D Everett Newell 8/26/2022

Mom

I've been watching you all my life
I watched your hard work
I watched your love of family
I'm thankful for traditions you set
The memories we made
Most, I'm thankful
God blessed me with you
Fly now Mom, Go be with Dad
You've earned your halo and wings
I hope to see you after a long
And desired tomorrow
Go safely and God speed
Your earned rewards await
We Love You Mom
We Love You!

D Everett Newell 2/26/2022

We lost you Mom on 2/20/2022

Moon Flower

Beautiful, mysterious you are
Avoiding day's sunlight
You awaken at dusk
Slowly as darkness sets
You unfurl your various petals
Opening wider and wider
Almost yelling, yes demanding
All take notice of your birth
You sit fully displayed in the
Sky lights, our heavens bow to you
Funny thing, found by accident
If alcohol blown on you
There is a false ejaculation
Nevertheless,
Given to a natural order
You open slowly,
You reign your Kingdom
Throughout the night
The morning ariscs, sadly
Bringing on you,
The moon flower's, demise

D Everett Newell 1/28/2022

More Than My Mom

As a Mom, she was the best
At her death, many consoled me
But no matter a crater in my heart remained
But you know she was much more
More than my Mom, her own identity
I don't ever want that to get lost
Please witness: As her story unfolds
She had her own private set of dreams
Born in 1933, her life encompassed so much
So many memories both good and bad
Loves, losses, trials and tribulations
Worked hard at home and outside
Jackson China, she made dishes
And to BF Goodrich, golf balls
Finishing her career at Fisher-Price
Where our work was child's play
Settling in as supervisor of a fab
A heart condition robbed her
She survived two triple heart bypasses
An aortic valve replacement,
Back and shoulder surgeries
So many days running on minimal sleep
My Mom was Dorothy Irene Carr Newell
Loving to travel as much as possible
Had a flair for painting
Loved to shop, dressed
Decorated with a fashion
Dad's best friend until he died
Forced to then forge a new life

Without him, I know it was hard
Most of all, her family was her life
Consuming us with that flame of embrace
Celebrated as a friend and
Revered family member to many
SO much value in a little woman
Such a brave noble fighter,
Even beat Covid, but Time
Coupled with Dementia, the long good-bye
Defeated her on a personal Alamo
You see, She was more than my Mom

D Everett Newell 5/2/2022

Morning Juxtaposition

I'm awake, aches and pain bark
Made it, I'm here for another day
Walking to bathroom, stretching, moving
Throwing on shorts and T-shirt
Swallowing my hot black coffee
Yeah, I can't use cream, my Mom didn't
It's the first of March. Spring is here
Sitting at the kitchen table I see
Brilliant blue skies, very crystal clear
I see many dogs being walked, birds sing
A high today in the 50's, air fresh
You have to feel rejuvenated, alive
But yet there remain reminders
As our Earth awakes from winter
Yesterday, blustery and snow with ice
Our lawn looked old covered in white
Two seasons erupting, exploding before me
Glorious to watch, to record
We who live in the US Northeast
Become accustomed to these four seasons
Yet do we really? Still a wonder
Winter leaves us grudgingly yet unwavering
Spring's rains and winds cleanse our world
A renewal, a rebirth every year
I've now lived through seventy of these
These seasonal hand-offs that mark time
Like rings on the trunk of a tree
They have shaped and aged me
So ending here, my thoughts written
Sharing right here and now
My morning juxtaposition

D Everett Newell 3/1/2024

Mountains Cry

On the highest hill
The one above the clouds
Almost to our spiritual heaven
Starts a chain reaction
Brilliant white snow awash
In God's brilliant sunlight
Sets things in motion
A melting occurs, bit by bit
Droplets become creeks as they run
Downward momentum carries them
They meet, becoming many rivers
Eroding earth, carving deep channels
A confluence where they flow
Together all dumping into vast oceans
Oceans that feed, nourish mankind
To think it all starts
On the highest of hills
As our mountains cry

D Everett Newell 5/5/2022

Mountains

Glistening flowing spring waters
The sun glares off your body
The mountain subtly tall, green
Dense with your many trees and hedgerows
I walk in the land God created
Possibly able to see deer, bear, elk, beaver
So lucky to be in this space
Luckier still, this is the home of my youth
Growing up among people who
Cherished this church of nature
Reflected in who they were
Hard working, simple lives
Clean, honest, building blocks
That set me on the path to who I am
These folks never took this for granted
Living in the valleys, protected
By these rolling rounded mountains

D Everett Newell 1/13/2022

Mr. Foxy

Your coat smooth
A red furry ball
Luscious tail, voluminous
Fast yet secret
Visiting us at dawn and dusk
Consistent for sure
Our security cameras give you none
We watch you sniff
Head down, going about
The business of finding
A family of rabbits under our deck
Not knowing you're admired
Part of nature's plan,
Keeping her balance
Your work tedious, bloody, a finality
Only killing to survive
There is nothing personal intended
Thankful we get to share
Watching you glide around
So delicate, balanced, pristine
Here is to you, our red fox
You're so fine, Mr. Foxy

D Everett Newell 1/28/2022

My Gift to All Dads for Fathers Day

My Heart Hurts

My heart hurts, yes it does
A weight has come over me
A state of mind that aches
Missing now many I loved
The last few years,
SO many losses stacked
Like firewood beside a cabin
Sitting by a metaphorical crystal creek
As the powerful waters rush by
It captures an image, my image
A droplet of water remains frozen
Poised near my eye,
Being a lone sentry to my soul
Some days it's very hard to move on
Wish I might see you all again
My loves, you remain within me
My testament to your lives
A saddle on the horse I will ride
Forever long, till my journey is done
I'll carry on remembering you
Sharing with all, I promise

D Everett Newell 4/12/2022

My Soul Soars

My soul soars with good news
All the darkness evaporated
Trials and tribulations laid aside
A renewed bounce in my step
Brighter blue shines in my eyes
I feel one with all in my world
My little universe, it's a day
Unlike any other, a first for me
Hearing my Great-grandchild's heartbeat
Yes, a great-grandchild
Pray he or she is healthy, the love
All that surround this baby will supply
This very lucky kid, born to us
A family rooted in love and history
DNA runs very deep, we are all
So very close, support runs integral
Can't believe I'm that old
But not about me, it's about us
Another mouth to feed, nurture, teach
The values we hold dear
Not those of others, we remain
A nuclear family, standing strong
Proud of each block that came
Before, and will come after
We know the secrets of family bonds
Standing strong, one unit
Against everything else, family first
My soul soars with good news
Thankful for another opportunity
To hold, protect another baby child

D Everett Newell 7/14/2023

My Wife Thinks, No I in This Team

Incredulous, hurtful, disappointing
My wife thinks "No I in this Team"
Complaining I don't do my share
Looking in the mirror
Knowing she is right
Needing to change this paradigm
Pitching in with dishes more
Trying to be a bigger part
Of regular household daily chores
Using my magic to move this needle
I get jiggy with it, I try
Bedazzling her with words
But this time, well most times
My words fail to impress
The look on her face, says
To no avail, a mind not changed
I failed at my quest
Getting that look, the one
That says to me direct
"There is no I in this Team"

D Everett Newell 2/7/2022

Nakoa

Always my quiet Grandson
So polite, willing to help
You're appreciated more than you know
From baseball to video gaming
Watching you grow from a boy
To now a young man
Taking on relationships
Being on your own
Amazing to me, how consistent
Steady your personality is
A subtle strength lies in you
Feelings of family, loyalty
Leader of peers, a great big brother
Koa, we are very proud of you
You're smooth son, smooth
Keep on your road, teaching us all
In your determined, yet understated ways
How to go about our lives
Thanks Buddy, for being you

D Everett Newell 2/1/2022

To Koa, Thank You Buddy, we love you

Neighborhood Nightmare

Lying in bed, windows open
Getting comfortable in my spot
Cool air wafting over me
I snuggle into my single bed cover
This will be a great night to sleep
I can't quite relax, I fidget, roll
At some point, seemed like hours
Drifting off, or I think I did
At least that's what the clock said
Upon my many frustrated glances
Suddenly, I hear a loud noise, focusing
Shocking intense,
Short intermittent blaring sounds
Not ambulance, firetruck, or police
Different, alarming, riveting, unnerving
Sitting up in bed, then standing up
Pausing to collect myself, then nervously
Wandering through our house
Slowly to the living room window
Looking out, I hear a deep vibration
A demonic growl
As if a tornado were baring down
Then I see very bright sparkling light
Phosphorus orange, red, blues, falling near
A huge object blasts past into the ground
A bounce and a boom between properties
Our two neighbors own,
It is here I awaken
I must go to the bathroom, but

I'm too afraid to move,
I am paralyzed
After this neighborhood nightmare

D Everett Newell 5/3/2022

New World

Many days looking at our world
I want to rip it a new asshole
Maybe it's just… my time is over
I'm now a dinosaur
Whose time has reached a logical conclusion
Much I see, read, hear
I just don't understand
Not wanting to offend gets harder
Each passing day we become
As a people, more isolated
Losing our compassion, and passions
For one another
There is a whole new playbook
I try to be a new me
Fitting into this puzzle of life
I round off my rough edges
Push myself into a place
Did I already say
I want to rip
This new world, a new asshole!

D Everett Newell 12/1/2021

Night Light

How many of you
In the middle of your very best dreams
Get an urgent message from the brain
Arriving in many ways, different stories
All ending with, 'Get to the bathroom!'
You quickly, dizzily sit up
Get your bearings, for that first step
One for me non-supportive and stiff
The saving grace always for me
Like a lighthouse on the ocean coast
Beckoning me, this way, into the white
Thanking God each and every time
For the critical placement of
Our night light

D Everett Newell 12/16/2021

No Blood Cells

Growing older no fun
Most simply, it sucks
Just found out
My bloodwork is funky
Doc said no worry yet
When I hear those words
My fears are alleviated
Well actually, not
Seems one in ten my age
Develops this problem
You see,
I have too many white blood cells
Coupled with too few red blood cells
Arthritis has crippled me
My eyesight and hearing fail
But the hell with it all
Onward I charge
Onward I write
Intrinsic to who I am
I need outlets to keep
This mind of mine engaged
My promise is
I'll continue to write
Till that time comes
When I'm called home
After I have no blood cells

D Everett Newell 2/2/2022

Ocean Baked

Out on the ocean, in a boat
Blue, turquoise, smooth water, I float

A day to relax, let my troubles go
Waves move me too far, time to row

Sun bearing down, hot and brightening
My skin reddens, I feel it tightening

Yet, I'm in no hurry to return
Time has stood still, I continue to burn

Lessons learned surely on this day
I know when done, I'll have to pay

Home now, trying to get to sleep
Turning side to side, pain emitted is deep

Morning now, as I slowly awake
Then I remember my yesterday when I baked

D Everett Newell 3/29/2022

Opportunities Missed

Sometimes our lives change
Events get derailed, begrudgingly
Bowing to things beyond our control
Picking ourselves up, to start again
The older I get, the harder to do
My hope for the future deflates
Oh, I still fight for tomorrow
But knowing the days ahead shrink
Both in number and quality
Don't feel sorry for me, really
It's the human condition, a road
We must all take to a conclusion
Join me in celebrating times
That we share because
They won't be replicated
Like a snapshot once taken
Never to be adjoined again
I'm ok with that, memories
They are our private memorials
To each other, cemented in souls
Now it bugs me when I can't join in
I accept the rest of this life
As I also accept a life after
There will be opportunities missed

D Everett Newell 12/6/2022

Orange

Juicy plump acidic sweet
You're all of this
Inside your sweet sections
Within membranes
Differ as people differ in shapes and sizes
Sometimes sweet, others sour
Rough outer cover, just waiting
For the correct one to peel us
Find our inner core, get to
A nectar unlike anything else
Why have just one
Sample and try the variety
That fits our personal taste
Be careful while selecting
A rotten one is found
Now and then, take it back
Don't buy a bad fruit
I promise if you dive in
Wholeheartedly, you'll be happy
Then I can ask
Orange you glad you did!

D Everett Newell 2/7/2022

O'Rorke

Paddy, did your parents know
Back in County Caven, Ireland
You'd become an American hero
Coming to Rochester, New York at one
Going to West Point
Then graduating 1861, 1st in class
Your life was short, but fame bright
For on that bloody hill
Little Round Top, sacrificing
Safety to protect the Union line
Being struck in the neck
Falling instantly dead, but you see
Paddy, you saved the Blue line
Rallied the troops, gave that
Last full measure, you will
Forevermore be a hero
And savior to Gettysburg
And the Union cause
A pride of Ireland
And the City of Rochester NY

D Everett Newell 12/16/2021

Over Yonder

Is it a human affliction
To want to be other
Than we are
Changing places with an actress
Getting the applause of star athletes
Acquiring the power of a politician
Maybe garner more love than a sibling
Standing here, I yearn for more
Of course, we all envy that of others
Here is a great caution
Do not ever allow this
To fester into the greens of jealousy
We really don't know
Someone else's life, do we
Unless we walk
That proverbial mile in their
Very old smelly worn shoes
I mean, how could we
Each of us fraught with free will
To walk our own stony paths
I'm asking you, be satisfied
With the life you created
Try not to look and compare
Over yonder!

D Everett Newell 1/31/2022
"Yep we all have it, varying degrees, varying reasons"

Pain

What do I mean, pain
Some the achy bone joint
Searing pain, from an arthritic war
Or dull one in the head
But also mental, also called
Anxiety, depression, sadness
Where you can't wait for day's end
You know, tomorrow's always better
But then it comes, and it's not
So hour by hour, by day
As weeks roll on you trick
Yourself into walking through
Your world, trying to hide it
From all you know
But ding-dong, or knocking on your door
Barging in again and again
I'm here, I'm moving in
Deal with me, learn to cope
With my forever friend, pain

D Everett Newell 12/14/2021

Pasta of My Past

Pasta of my past
So yummy, good, simple is best
Like ziti or thin spaghetti
Covered in a rich red sauce
Made with time, love, and care
Starting with two pork chops
Italian sausage, meatballs
All browned with garlic
A perfection to your senses
Stirring in the tomato paste
This base welcoming the next
Many tomato sauces, building
A crescendo of flavor, to
Pour over soft noodles of choice
My mouth waters at this
As I read, my nostrils flare
Man, the imaginary smells
Only thing left is to grate
Cheese on top of this bubbling mound
Umm, so good, The Pasta of my past

D Everett Newell 12/1/2021
Dedicated to Ange Bonito, who made the best Pasta I've ever tasted!

Perception To Reality

Started out hairy, ragged
Beard bushy, full of holes
My mustache thick brown, silver, red
Thinking I'll trim it
So, cutting off beard I slip
Oh no, thinking, oh well
I'll cut more, shape it
Oh no, I slip again
OK, the beard comes off
Now to the stache, slowly chip away
Whoops, oh no, I slipped again
Damn arthritic hands, I decide
It comes off now
So my face is trim, my head bald
Looking in the mirror, nice
Trim, clean, shiny I expect
Oh no, what I see
Startles me, looking back at me
A face I remember
Is Mr. Potato Head!!
Changing my perception to reality

D Everett Newell 12/14/2021

Pheromones & Crushes

It's a funny notion
As a young person
Feeling attractions for the first time
A conception thrust upon us
Puberty reigning suddenly efficiently
The girl next door suddenly is not
Becoming an image for moving on
Nature's way of bridging us
As procreation is why we are here
To keep our species alive
No matter however way it's sliced
Like polar opposite magnets we are drawn
Much like moths to flames
How many of us had crushes
Not reciprocated, ones unknown
Pheromones and crushes
A cruel mix that thrills or hurts us
Part of the plan as we grow
Total eclipse of our hcart
Weaving through our beings
To be remembered always!

D Everett Newell 11/3/2022

Pills

Commercials on TV
Would have us believe
We each could be superhuman
Pills for every conceivable occasion
Illness disappears, as easily ingested
If you're short, get taller
If sick, get well
Only $19.95 each, a bargain
Each bottle harnessing nature's powers
If acting now you get
Two for one, a BOGO
A Bargain unleashing rainbows of health
Coming in all shapes and colors
Heard just today, yes it's true
Using just one
To put back your Va Va Voom!
So why not join in
How can we justify not
Pills, pills, pills, pills
More pills, nothing to fear
Break out those credit cards
Order yours today, tomorrow
Pills, Pills, Pills, Pills

D Everett Newell 11/9/2022

Please, One Holiday at a Time

It's Halloween, we are fully engaged
Goblins, witches, ghosts at our door
Shopping for Halloween candy
It's marked down now
Christmas holiday now on display

It's Christmas, we are fully engaged
Jesus, Santa, gifts, family, love
Shopping for last-minute gifts
It's marked down now
Valentine's Day now on display

It's Valentine's, we are fully engaged
Chocolate candy, hearts, cupid, signs of affection
Shopping for a last-minute card
Most shelves now are changed
Easter is now on display

I ask, it's a pet peeve
Rushing us always, I refuse to resign
Please, Please, One Holiday at a Time

D Everett Newell 12/16/2021

Power of Us

Singly we are ok
Left to our own journeys
We manage just fine
Conquering all in our path
The many pebbles, rocks, stones
But given time, they chip away
We become a bit bent and scratched
In time, an erosion takes place
Can't be helped or stopped
Years wear away, but yet
Our family and friends provide
A shield to protect us
Holding in a collective bosom
Of hugs, smiles, and more
Building us up once again
Giving us fuel to fight on
Living our each day fully
We have a strength intrinsic
Deep within each of us
Yet we do feel alone at times
Enjoying us, beats that always
Numbers provide a new power
Continuing our climb through life
Gathering, we become a bigger one
Shielding us from the meteors of living
I'll always be thankful
To my personal tribe, who
Stand beside me always, guiding me
On my journey, I'm thankful
I have this power of us!

D Everett Newell 7/4/2023

Pretzel Logic

Life with all its twists
Many turns, full of surprises
Good and bad coupled together
To give a dish best revered
No two days are ever alike
Safe to say, no minute or hour
Change is always at our door
Ringing, knocking to be let in
It's how we manage the onslaught
Sometimes we run, others we charge
At times instinct kicks in
Coin toss at any unbridled moment
Yet there are parallels
That act out without our recognition
Making our sojourn different
Unpredictable, unique unto us all
Panic is slain with our vitality
A predestined code to live
To stay alive, stay upright
You see, I think our existence
Is much like that of a pretzel
The curves, bends, it can be salty

D Everett Newell 6/15/2023

Putin

When will you have enough
You are a maniac destroyer of life
Blood in the streets
Homes burn, lives ruined
People fleeing in droves
When will you have enough
Crying, screaming, people in pain
Because of your greed
Men from two countries killing
Not even understanding why
Horrors unfold in your name
When will you have enough
Alarming all people who care
Ruthlessly changing geographic boundaries
Blatantly causing damage everywhere
Putin, You are Satan
Putin, You are deranged
Putin, You will pay!
Your hubris sickens me
Putin, hope you rot in Hell!

D Everett Newell 2/25/2022

Rainbows from Waterfalls

Rainbows from waterfalls
Transcend a peace within
Our souls cry in happiness
The sun’s bright beams shine through
As the heavenly vapors quickly
Bend prisms of colors
Cascading us with warmth
The water soothes our bodies
And the intrinsic link to our hearts
Angels find their haloes
When they swirl beneath
Then taking their loving flights
A simple process bringing peace
Ringing bells, chimes, harpsichords
And the music from all
Bathe us in a secure womb
That protects our peace
Our very own well-being
Always be delighted and very thankful
For the rainbows from waterfalls

D Everett Newell 12/6/2022

Random Thoughts

Life never promised
Its seldom we think on that
Each day is fragile
Tomorrows are fleeting
As the winds move clouds
People here today
Could be gone in a flash
Evaporated in the steams of living
On the morrow, live hard
Love hard, nurture all you encounter
Then try to remember it all
Don't squander moments
Each is precious, in so many ways
Sometimes realizations are not realized
Don't live as to regret
Don't be afraid to dive in, live
See you can die, even while taking breath
Apathy can kill,
But empathy surely will heal

D Everett Newell 3/7/2022

Record of Man

In heaven, going over daily tallies
A record so to speak, that of man
Counting both good and bad
Heaven's pearly gates dim a bit
Disappointed, frowns emit
This can't be correct, an angel
Is heard exclaiming to another
13,000 nuclear warheads on Earth
434 million guns, just in the US
The human race has indeed grown
Yet we need more love and compassion
Fewer people attend churches
Or for that matter,
Believe in a higher power
The nuclear home is broken
Torn down by distance and academia
Parents respect by the youth, eroded
Sure, man does a lot that is virtuous
But is that enough to tip our scales
Man has intrinsic nature to do wrong
They can't help being this killing engine
Not at all what was intended
Depressing at times, this "Record of Man"

D Everett Newell 2/26/2022

Red Chariot

I'm amazed and bewildered
Being a person of limited mobility
Walking cement floors for 40 years
Had not been kind, arthritis's friend
The very best and worst of people
When I'm upon my plastic steed
The seas sometimes part as if
I were Moses, as they politely
Let me pass, friendly, compassionately
Then the others who play this game
Liking to play tag with me
At the last second, jumping in front
Giving me three choices, to break
To swerve, or to run them over
Now if this happens on a
Inclined trail or path
This becomes quite a feat
Gravity pulls me back, so unlikely
To be hitting the brakes
Swerving the only option
Just missing people as I go, or
Worst case, brushing them in passing
Getting that look, as if
I'm responsible for their stupidity
Carrying on, I applaud the
Helpful, chagrin for the others
Stay out of the way of my Red Chariot

D Everett Newell 1/25/2022

Rekindle

How does one rekindle a fire
A friendship that burned out
Yet, in your heart you know
Its importance to all you are
We assimilate ourselves from others
Growing into a spirit and soul
That is with us til the light goes out
Needed is that phoenix to rise
Burn brightly once again, a fuel
To finish off the trek left to walk
Be willing to forget past woes
The cracks that widened over time
Ones truly not remembered yet
Divided us, left us without each other
With a gentle nudge or push
A rekindle begins with the extended hand
Remembering what made us before
Being that, steadfastly again

D Everett Newell 4/7/2023

Dedicated to my friend Alana

Reversal Of

I had a dream
Red was green, green was red
Cats were dogs, dogs were cats
I had a dream
Chocolate was vanilla, vanilla was chocolate
Night was day, day was night
I had a dream
Old was young, young was old
Light was dark, dark was light
I had a dream
Life was death, death was life
Gas was electric, electric was gas
I had a dream
Cars were planes, planes were cars
Up was down, down was up
My dream enlightened me while
Scaring me, rethinking all
When I woke up, calmed down
I thought what was this
A glimpse to our future
Where our way of life
Everything, was not as it was
Now a reversal of

D Everett Newell 6/4/2023

Roller Coaster

My life has become a roller coaster
Which when younger I enjoyed
As I grow older
And the “Dips” become more frequent
I only find myself wanting OFF!
The shrieks of thrills
Have turned into angry shouts
Beyond the point of reason

Judy Wolford Pierannunzio

Say a Little Prayer

Needing more love
As well as peace of mind, body, spirit
I lay me down tonight
Hoping for a better tomorrow
Hoping to make many more
Of the kind of memories
That touch our hearts and souls
We each get one life to live
Praying we don't squander it
Also with hope others don't do it for us
Reach out to our lonely
Embrace all kinds of humanity
We must walk this trail together
Failing that, life becomes meaningless
As I do lay me down tonight
Counting my blessings
And wishing all many more
I'll say a little prayer

D Everett Newell 12/1/2021

Scared

I quit being a child
At 23 when my son Corey
Came bounding into my world
The partying, motorcycle riding
Some of the reckless carefree died
Hitting me hard, a new load of maturity
I was now responsible for another life
Really, I was too young, not
The best Dad, Father I could be
My hope at best was I'd improve
Feeling guilty, the immediate love
Did not wash me in its totality
What I felt more, was fear
You know what, I quickly grew
Into this role of protector and advocate
Today, no one I love more than Corey
And my daughter Alissa, who came
Two years after, I'd be a better father today
Than I ever was back then
In the beginning, I was a kid myself
Sorry I was not better, but
We all survived, both my kids
Are better parents than I ever was

D Everett Newell 6/16/2023

Shades of Gray

Growing up
We had our heroes
Maybe my youth was naive
Possibly misspent daydreaming
I sat and learned from my TV
Men like John Wayne,
Tuff guys, Western cowboys
Possessing a definitive line of integrity
Reading novel after novel
Like the writings
Of the great J.R.R. Tolkien
Books that were a classic
Didactic to the Nazi's
And the Great Wars in Europe
Reading comic after comic
Where Batman, Superman
Always conquered darkness
Attacked and defeated
Evil at every turn
The world, my world,
Then was black and white
Good always won against bad
Today, things are muddled
So confusing, troubling
Our enemies, allies switch daily
Who exactly can any of us trust?
Even both ends
Of our government corrupt

I long for simpler clearer times
Now the world is made up of many
Shapes, types, shades of gray

D Everett Newell 8/31/2022

Silly Fun

Laughing at anything stupid
Always the Clown
Chuckles would be proud
The group hit its stride
After years of togetherness
We became a unit, knowing well
Each and all our individual parts
Jelled as one movement
Our humor evolved
Engrained through assimilation
Even filling in thoughts
Where no words needed expression
As a whole we understood
Glints in individual's eyes
Leading to many wide-eyed grins
Lightness in the shared air
Made for great moments
A group of friends evolved
Through their shared experiences
Forever like riding a bike
Immediately find their defined grove
Nothing comes close
To the simplest of happy times
Times we shared silly fun

D Everett Newell 11/20/2022

Silver Tree with a Colored Wheel

A late fall road trip
Had excited the whole family
The four of us were ready
Western New York to West Virginia
Not a long drive
As long drives go
A good time was to be made
Looking forward to good country
Sounds of old at the Jamboree
In Wheeling, a music city
Arriving Friday just in time to eat
Then off to explore the many window fronts
On these quaint and holiday streets
Mom saw something on display
That drew her in,
Like a moth to a brilliant flame
The look she gave us,
 Beckoned we follow
There it stood
In all of its shiny newness
For you see, because of me
My allergies kept our family
From traditional live Christmas trees
Back then, artificial were
Mostly silver some pink,
Usually not representative
Of a real live Scotch Pine
Because of Mom's passion,
Her momentary vision

This one was special,
Along with the stiff bright aluminum
There came a rotating color wheel
Which strobed,
As it washed every inch
With many bright hues
Changing its very sterile appearance
And there was more
Coming also with a small blower
And a tray, and octopus' arms
Enabling fake snow to fly and pop
Mom was so happy, her face glowing
Her smiles becoming infectious
As we all started to grin
Tears well up thinking of the moment
It was now a part of us
The memories of it, lasting till now
Our silver tree, with a colored wheel

D Everett Newell 11/9/2021

Silver Balls

I

Well, my memoir starts during the early days of World War II. As an older brother, I wanted to enlist, but my ailing father made my mother insist that I stay and help keep the bakery going. That became a moot point when the draft notice arrived. The youngest in the family must now take over.

I was excited, yet scared, a mix of emotions. I'd never been outside of our little valley, let alone in another country, in a different part of the world. What made it easier, it was now a done deal. I had no choice.

On a grey rainy morning, I boarded the bus, which would take me to my training bus. After eight grueling weeks, we were ready; well, were we? Our outfit being deemed ready, we flew to the East coast, the next steps, a ship to our staging area in Europe!

Like all good Americans, we were in the swing of saving pretty much everything for the war effort, including grease, gas, meat, and tinfoil. In the Army, it was no different, and I took up the habit of wadding the tinfoil wrappers from cigarette and gum packages and placing them in the breast pocket of my field jacket.

The war took us from England to Sicily, then Italy. It played havoc with my head. During combat, the enemy was just that, not sons, brothers, fathers.

Post-combat, when we would march through the battered villages and towns, street urchins would come out like rabbits from warrens and shout, "Americaners! You got gum, Joe?" And we did. Gum, like cigarettes, was always a part of our C-rations. So, I would open the foil from a stick and eager fingers would snatch it away. Naturally, I wadded the foil and stuck it in my pocket.

After a while, I found the wads and rolled them all together into a ball. When a sphere was about the size of a tennis ball, I placed it in my pack. Other members of my company noticed what I was doing, and it became a sort of thing; everyone was saving tinfoil. When my friend Joe was shot at Salerno and sent back, he gave me his ball and said, "It's yours, you know what to do with it!"

Well, I didn't! Soon, I had several balls in my pack and the weight was beginning to tell. Of course, there was no such thing as recycling in the field, so I was at a loss at what to do with the silver spheres. Apparently, this was a problem with a number of the company, and no one wanted to be the first to ask me what to do.

Finally, just north of Naples, a BAR man we called Jonesy came right out and asked, "Well, Jaime-boy, what are we going to do with this stuff?" I called a small conference and we decided to stack our collected balls in a wooden ammo box and bury it with honors, wrapped in a tattered American flag. What someone would think of such a casket if found in the future would be anyone's guess.

We decided this would be a good policy to follow throughout our mainland venture and we deposited three more caches before duty took us elsewhere. The war, thank God, came to a close. We all, with much anticipation, looked forward to going home. There were several silver balls still underway which made the trip with us.

We arrived stateside and home was parades with tickertape and maidenly kisses, children waving flags to the tunes of brass bands. Then, reality set in.

I got on with my life, finding a full-time job. I then chased a young lady down the street until she finally caught me! Joanie and I were married the twenty-fifth of December 1946. Yeah, I know, who gets married on Christmas? Well, we did! The next step was finding that proverbial white house, picket fence and all. It was located up on a hill, near the small valley in which I grew up.

We were settling in when the silver ball came again to my attention. It sat there in my palm, a little smaller than a baseball, glistening, crinkled and wrinkled, and I did not know what to do with it. Even though my wife said, “The war’s over; get rid of it,” I was loath to do it. The tinfoil had come so far with me and seemingly taken on a meaning of its own, whatever it was.

I placed it on our fireplace mantle. My other half looked at it and sighed. “Well, the least you can do is smooth it out,” and stomped off. I took it down and rolled it in my palms. This would take a while, I thought. So, I took to showing the ball to all our visitors, inviting them to roll it around in their palms, smoothing it out. Our kids, of which we had three, took to the task almost immediately, and over the years, the silver ball became smooth, like a great silver ball bearing. It shined there on the fireplace mantle, as if it truly belonged, which I guess it did. Even the wife took on a sort of possessive joy and would, herself, point it out to visitors, telling its story.

II

Over the years, a few of us veterans stayed in contact, and wouldn’t you know it, they also kept their own tinfoil balls and had them placed in honored settings in their homes.

I had lost touch with Jonesy for a number of years when he surprised me with a letter. He had not been as blessed as I and had trouble integrating himself back into American society. He drank and had a temper, not a good mix, and often found himself jobless or in trouble. Then, his father died, and he took over the family business, which I never did understand exactly what it was. Anyway, it apparently settled him down and … well, this is his tale.

He and his wife were asleep one evening when he awoke to the sound of glass breaking. He cautioned his wife to stay where she was and be quiet. Then, picking up his baseball bat which he always kept next to the bed for just such an occasion, moved into the living room. There were two burglars, wearing low slouch caps, with eyes blackened with grease. He brandished the bat and said, “drop what you have and get out of here!”

The crooks were astonished! One immediately ran out through the front door. But the other was not to be put off and he pulled a knife. The two men were about even in size and strength, and Jonesy got too close, and in order to avoid being cut, had to drop the bat. The crook grinned a broken-tooth grin and said, "Now, I got ya!"

Jonesy glanced around and noticed his ball of foil on the table next to him, displayed under a glass cover. He quickly lifted the cover, grabbed the ball and, like it was a hand grenade, or maybe the third-strike pitch at Wrigley, he caught his adversary squarely in the right blackened eye.

He grabbed the knife and twisted the crook about and threw him out the door. He closed the door and locked it, noticing a broken glass pane. It had been broken to allow an arm to be inserted and unlock the door. Picking up the silver ball, he kissed it and carefully placed it back on the table under its glass cover. He left the knife beside it. Tomorrow he'd fix the pane in the door .... maybe replace the door altogether. Now, he was going back to bed.

On awakening in the morning, Jonesy went to the room that housed his silver ball. His ball was sitting in its place of honor but there was no knife. Even more startling, no windows were broken, in fact there were no signs of a break-in. Jonesy was taken aback, and slowly sat down in his favorite recliner, lit his favorite cigar, and began to sort out in his mind what had happened. Jonesy decided right there at that moment's intersection, he'd reach out to me, and a few others. He had to know if he was going crazy, or if there was something else at work here.

I was just sitting down for supper and the phone rang. I picked it up, heard a very nervous, "Hi Jaime, it's me, Jonesy!" He wanted to know if I still had a ball of foil, if I had anything odd happen to me, or if I knew if any of the others had. He suggested that somehow, maybe there was an energy left behind in the balls, something intrinsic to each. We both at this point were intrigued. We really had no answers, but we knew we wanted to find some. I had some time to spare so I made arrangements to take my silver ball and visit Jonesy. Maybe together we could sort out what was happening.

The two silver spheres sat side-by-side on the kitchen table, one a little less smooth and slightly smaller than the other. My wife and I sat opposite Jonesy and his wife. We had just related the history of the foil balls to our wives and rehashed the break-in story. Both wives were skeptical. Jonesy's wife, her name was Marion, knew of the break-in of course, hearing the noise, but had never left the bed until morning and had only his version.

***

I said I had a story to relate, which I had never told anyone for fear of being thought crazy. Just a little while after our first child was born, another of our buddies, a man named Cranston … he had been our platoon Corporal … called me and told me of his silver ball.

It seems that he had finally been about to throw the thing away. He had no use for it and no attachment to it; it had just been something he had carried around, like his rifle. He lived single in a great city, which he hated, but it was where he could find work. He had thought of throwing the ball into some machine, or at some cop, or something to disrupt the world. Then, he figured the trouble which that would involve was not worth any pleasure derived, so he decided to throw it into the river.

Early one morning, he had reached the center and highest portion of one of the city's great bridges and had just pulled the foil ball out of his field jacket pocket when there was a terrible crash and he spun around. A bus had been side-swiped by some motorist and knocked off its course. It was heading straight for him.

He tried to climb the railing, but it was so damp with dew, all his feet did was slip. He faced the bus, which showed no sign of slowing, and he threw the foil ball at it. A totally stupid and irrational act of defiance. The next second he was still on the bridge, but traffic moved along as if nothing had happened. The bus was slowing, moving on down the road. The foil ball had disappeared.

He called me, knowing my attachment to the silver balls, and told me the tale. I figured he was probably drunk. In any case, I thanked him and forgot about it. Cranston died a month later of a heart attack. I was shocked and felt bad about not taking his story seriously; I did not go to the funeral.

Three faces stared at me across the table. We needed to figure out a plan on where to go next. Do we reach out to other known silver ball holders? In doing so, would we alarm them? Would they even listen to us? I mean, what we have witnessed is truly strange.

"Right," I said to myself more than to the group.

Jonesy and both wives finally, after dead silence, started talking, and as a group we decided to reach out to others who hold these foil balls. First, we would need a list of the men who might have brought back silver balls, then find out where they now live. After our unit left Europe, we migrated throughout the country.

We started making calls and compiling addresses. Surprisingly, it turned out to be a pretty small list. Next, we decided Jonesy and I would go on the road to reach out, while our wives stayed at home compiling any data we sent back. We would look at what we had, looking for any patterns that may show us what the hell was going on.

III

Jonesy and I began in Gettysburg, Pennsylvania where Bob, a buddy from our unit lived. To be honest, none of us knew his real last name. Some called him Bobby Sheetz for no apparent reason. This would be a great place to commence our hunt. I mean, a silver ball with paranormal traits in one of the most haunted places in the world – Gettysburg! What could be better?

I remember Bob kept us up all night sometimes, regaling us with ghost tales about his hometown. And wouldn't you know it, he now runs a ghost tour business in Gettysburg. We caught our flight to Baltimore, Maryland, rented a car, and drove the one hour to Gettysburg. As we closed in, statues, cannons, and memorial markers of the Civil War battle popped up along the countryside.

Bob, "not Robert or Roberto", had been well-liked within the squad and I looked forward to seeing him again. However, when we entered the dusty doors of 'Historic by Day and Ghost by Night Tours' a strange young man with a thick southern accent informed us that Bob was away doing research. He told us that his name was Dariant Brown, that he was Bob's partner, and asked if there was anything he could help us with.

Jonesy said, "I seem to remember Bob mentioning you … not during the War but since … perhaps on the phone. You seem awful young to have been in the war."

"Wa'l, age can be deceptive," replied Dariant, and he asked again, "how can I help?"

I spoke up, "We have a problem, no, not really a problem, but a mystery, about balls of foil we collected during the war. It seems strange things have been going on." I smiled, "I don't know if you believe in the supernatural or ghosts …"

"Gentlemen," Dariant spoke softly, "this IS Gettysburg. Look at the name of our business. Oh yes, we know about ghosts and manifestations and such."

He broke off and walked over to an ancient desk; the fireplace was behind it. Dariant pointed to the mantle over the fireplace. "Ah believe that is Bob's foil ball." There, glistening in the dim light, was a foil ball, a tad larger than my own, but rolled so smooth as if to be a single piece, looking for all the world like a small silver cannon ball.

Jonesy moved over and looked carefully at the sphere, then asked if he could pick it up.

"Ah suppose that would be all right," said Dariant, "It's just sat there for ages gathering dust." However, when Jonesy picked it up, I could see no trace of dust at all. Whereas our balls were interesting to look at, this one was fascinating. It drew the eye and seemed to absorb it.

I asked, "Has anything strange occurred dealing with the ball? Any mysterious phenomena?"

"Wait!" said Jonesy. "Jaime-boy, we need to bring this gent up to date. How can he help us if he doesn't know what's been going on?"

He turned to Dariant, "Would you like to hear our story, actually two or three stories? Perhaps over a meal? We've been traveling a while and could use a refresher. Bring Bob's ball; you've shown us yours, we'll show you ours."

Over bowls of steaming French Onion Soup at the Dobbin House Tavern, we unfolded our stories within stories. The three foil balls set together between us.

When Jonesy and I had finished our narrative, we looked at Dariant.

He looked us both in the eye, then smiled and said, "Fascinating … a good word that I learned from Bob … but not surprising. Everything is connected, animate, inanimate; the events of our lives affect not only ourselves and the people around us, but also the things."

Leaning back, he stretched long arms over his head with a sigh and continued, "I could not begin to tell you of the things I have seen or even know about. I am tied to Gettysburg because of this. However, I know nothing about Bob's ball of foil. I can tell you that he always kept it in sight and seemed almost afraid of it. I did ask him once about it and he merely said that the ball was of a time best forgotten."

Picking it up and feeling it in his palm, Dariant said, "It does feel alien … different from anything I have ever felt. I will try to contact Bob on your behalf but that may be difficult. He usually only works three months out of the year. We hire guides for the rest of the time and I fill in when I happen to be around."

He arose and thanked us for bringing him the tales and promised to contact us by phone if he learned anything else; then he was gone. We found out our meal had been paid for, and when we went back to the tour shop, it was locked with a large CLOSED sign on the door.

***

We had booked rooms at the Gettysburg Best Western, which, as luck would have it, was right across the road from the Soldiers' National Cemetery. As fascinating as talking with Dariant was, we were tired, so we retreated to our rooms and we both had a very deep sleep that night. Awaking the next morning, we showered, shaved, grabbed a bite to eat and coffee. We returned to meet up with Dariant at their shop.

We had a few more questions to ask Dariant, but before we had a chance to ask, Dariant said something that shocked us. He had something to share with us that he had been reluctant to say earlier, without checking with Bob. After we left him yesterday, he had somehow contacted Bob, so he was eager to share this morning. He told us to grab our rental car and meet him out in front of the shop.

Dariant jumped into the car with us, giving Jonesy directions to drive to an area near the Eisenhower farm. He told us to stop at an old, abandoned, bridge the locals call "suicide bridge", supposedly a place with a lot of paranormal activity lingering near and around the steel span. Fable has it a few people had hung themselves at this spot. Dariant walked slowly to a mound of dirt on the side of a worn trail. Bending down, taking the earth in his hands, he almost willed the dirt to move. Then we saw what looked like wood. As more dirt disappeared, a small wooden ammo box came into view, with rotted threads which we knew had once been an American flag.

I said, "no way, this can't be possible," but it was.

A coffin we had buried in Europe, was now here in Gettysburg, Pennsylvania. On opening it, we saw it was indeed filled with those damn silver balls!

Stunned, not knowing what to do next, we thanked Dariant and took the cache of balls back to the store. We went back to our list of comrades and checked the next name, actually the last name, on our list, Damien Calpepper.

IV

Damien had been vertically challenged, actually too short for enlistment, but in times of war, he was in. We called him "Imp" as he was always pulling practical jokes and coming up with terrible puns. Yet, in times of distress, chaos, and depression, he gave our squad its sense of humor. He kept us moving when the rest of us would have given up. He was our spur, our prod, and we hated and loved him for it.

The last time I had seen Damien Calpepper was in a make-shift poker game in an alley outside of Macy's, New York City, during our glorious return home from the war. Our investigation had turned up an address for him, twenty years old. Incredibly it was just down the road in Baltimore.

We called Joanie and Marion, informing them of what we had seen and what we were going to do, and started back to Baltimore. As we were driving down Hwy 15 to pick up I-70, Jonesy asked me what I remembered about Damien.

"Well, he never seemed to be very literate, but he was a nut about Edgar Allen Poe. Knew all the stories and seemed fascinated by the idea that Poe believed in an inner earth."

Jonesy was silent for a moment and then asked, "Didn't Poe live in Baltimore?"

"Yes… I think so. He died there." I replied.

Jonesy went on, "I remember reading that Poe had few friends and many enemies, was involved in alcohol and drugs … and married his underage cousin."

"Well," I said, "the many enemies part may explain some of the rest. Hard to fight back when you are dead."

I continued, "Besides his poetry and stories, I remember he was a literary critic, certainly a job to create enemies. He died young and lived during the early 1800s. That's all I got about Poe."

Jonesy laughed, “What does that have to do with Calpepper?”

“Probably nothing,” I replied.

***

Like most cities east of the Mississippi, Baltimore is old, very old … not European old where ancient ruins shine in the sun. The American old, shiny, modern, multi-colored images of Baltimore seen on TV and shown to tourists, conceal a dark and dank level of history underneath. Cobblestone and rot, shadows and a myriad of odors, pleasing and not-so-much, capture the imagination and sends it down narrow, twisting streets, past old brick and wooden multi-level structures, lying eyeless and unkempt. It is hard to tell whether the remaining fences or the structures themselves, are actually leaning.

It was down one of these buried and unspoken-of streets we found Damien’s address. There was a street sign, which was not on our brand-new city map, and we had to stop a couple of times to ask directions. There were no numbers on any of the buildings.

An abandoned brick factory stood opposite a shaky row of five homes; four being two level and the one in the middle, three level. This was odd and gave the block the appearance of rising in the middle. This idea was furthered by the fact that each house out from the middle one seemed shabbier and more run down than the last. Only the middle structure had seen any paint in the last 50 years and, though cracked, it seemed to still have all of its windows in place.

Though no numbers were visible, it was apparent that only the middle structure was inhabited. The others were knee deep in grass and weed, bore broken and missing widows, two had caved-in doors and one, no door at all. The real tell was the mailbox. This style of home, if it had a mailbox at all, as opposed to a slit in the door, usually had them on the wall next to the door. This one had a normal mailbox on a stake set out from the door. It was black and the extra-large size for parcels. On top was a statue of a large raven.

Jonesy said, "I take it, this is the place."

Some locks unlatched and Damien Calpepper opened the door with a .44 magnum revolver in his right hand.

Surprisingly, he looked the same as back when, maybe shorter, if possible. His face was grizzled, unshaven enough to look unkempt yet not quite a beard. His eyes still bore the excitement which they always had.

"Jaimie, Jonesy! What the blue blazes are you doing here?" He motioned us in and locked the door, a triple lock, behind us.

"It's the tinfoil spheres, isn't it?" He placed the revolver on the top of a stack of books. "You're here about those dag-nab silver balls. I know you are! It all makes sense." He hustled us into a sitting room, perhaps once called a parlor, not what I would call a living room. It was cluttered with books, many opened, and charts and maps, folded and unfolded, newspapers, and many, many notes written on old Red Chief pads. He swept a couple of chairs clean and said, "Sit down. We have a lot to talk about. I am so glad to see you! I never thought … but then, we didn't, did we … nor did we know …"

He then got us up again, and led us into another room. There, above a fireplace which looked like it hadn't seen use in the last 100 years or so, sat a dozen or so silver balls, in various sizes and degrees of smoothness.

"These," he gestured, "popped up. Just popped up out of nowhere on the mantel, over the period of the last month or so. I really didn't pay attention. I rarely use this room. Actually, I don't really even know this house. About six months ago, my condo … bizarre story, same address as this but on the other side of town … well, it was broken in to and an old woman was killed and then the whole building was set on fire. That week, get this, I received a letter in the mail telling me that I inherited this house from a passing relative by the name of Valdemar. Well, of course, I immediately knew that was bogus … you remember the Poe story?"

We looked at him blankly.

"However," he continued, "when I checked with the Lawyer, they had the deed, and everything was legal and proper. I moved in here. The house is so intimidating, I have been too afraid to even go up to the third level and never got off the landing of the second.

Since then, I have been researching everything I can to understand what has been going on. When it did dawn on me … the silver balls, I got worried. I bought the gun and new locks and here I am.

The few neighbors in the area call this 'The Poe House' because of the mailbox. I wish I could take credit for that, but it was already here.

I need a drink! You guys? I want to talk with you."

We moved back into the original room and reseated ourselves. Damien had found a half-empty bottle of brandy somewhere and three unmatched coffee cups which he half filled. Mine said, 'McDonalds'.

Calpepper leaned forward and asked, "Did you ever hear of Franz Mesmer?"

Jonesy spoke up, "The man who invented hypnosis?" I looked at him, astonished.

"Sort of …" Damien went on, "he believed there was an invisible force in all living creatures, loosely called 'animal magnetism', which could connect everything living. In Poe's story, it connected even past death."

I spoke up, "I don't remember Poe's story but what does Mesmer … hypnosis, have to do with our silver balls?"

"Forget hypnosis, Jaime! It's the connect between things. Some Mesmerists believe that force, that connection, extends to all things, animate and inanimate." He sat back and stared at us while our minds took this in.

I began, “Damien, do you remember our buddy Bob we served with?” Jaime nodded his head in the affirmative. “Well, we visited him and his partner Dariant in Gettysburg before we headed here.”

“Go on,” said Damien.

“Well, you know Bob, he is ever-elusive, one minute here, the next gone.”

“Yeah,” Damien murmured.

“Well anyway, his partner Dariant showed us the darndest thing.” Jonesy and I continued to tell Damien about following Dariant out on the battlefield at Gettysburg, to the area that time forgot, where not many tourists venture, to what the locals call Suicide Bridge. We described how Dariant had showed us the wooden case of those silver balls, buried in the ground there.

Damien just looked at us, with that wide-eyed, ‘no-that-can’t-be’ look.

As a group we decided to take the silver balls from Damien’s mantel with us, and head back to Gettysburg and put all the balls together. We couldn’t make any sense of this, but felt we were being driven by something greater here. Very possibly Mesmer’s theory was playing out, as it must!

Jonesy spoke up, “Hey, while we are here, I’ve always wanted to see Poe’s gravesite.”

Damien said, “Let’s get things packed up, and I will go there with you on your way out of town.” Everyone nodded in agreement, and we made our way to the cemetery on Fayette Street.

Grabbing a map at the Gate House, we drove directly to Poe’s grave. We noticed one red rose, decaying as it lay at the base of the stone. Also, while paying our respects, we saw a freshly disturbed square patch of dirt on the side of the memorial stone. Of course, curiosity got to us, and we moved the fresh soil. To our great dismay, we uncovered two more silver balls.

We were stunned but decided to bring these balls along with us and get back to Gettysburg and join up with Dariant and Bob again.

The three of us were quiet and somber after our meeting at the Gravesite; each of us lost in our own thoughts. We headed back to Gettysburg in silence, ending up on RT 15 North, back to the signs, monuments, cannons, and Bob and Dariant!

V

We sat haphazardly inside the 'Historic by Day and Ghost by Night Tours', in the same room with the fireplace, on mis-matched dining room chairs, an old stuff chair, and a wooden crate. Jonesy and I, Damien, Dariant, and Bob had shown up, which made us all feel better in that he always seemed to have a better handle on stuff historic and strange.

Though midday, the store sign was turned to "Closed" and the blinds were drawn. We had telephoned Joanie and Marion and invited them to come, but they had consulted each other and decided that whatever was going on had to do with the war and the "boys", so they merely said, "Keep us informed."

"Gentlemen," began Bob, "it seems to me that we are dealing with a manifestation, perhaps akin to what Mesmer and Damien were thinking. Somehow, our balls of tinfoil have followed us through space and time. Maybe the magic of Gettysburg, and even some of the stuff Poe was into, may also have something to do with it.

The real question is, what are we going to do, if anything?"

"Well," spoke up Jonesy after a brief silence, "I guess we should collect them; they all seem to be coming to us, anyway … maybe put them together, in a museum like Bob's here."

Bob replied, "I admit I like the idea of studying the balls; they seem to have incredible properties attached to them. Perhaps Damien's Poe House would work better though?"

I spoke up, "But Bob, what is happening? Is there any explanation?"

"Oh yes," he said, "possibly many explanations. We know that metal is a conductor of energy. If Mesmer was right, and every human being puts out energy, a tiny bit could be absorbed into each and every piece of those silver balls."

"And the weird manifestations or whatever," I continued, "what about them?"

"You've got me there, Jaime. We are not even sure what ghosts are. Mesmer's ideas could even be a base for them. My guess is that if a little bit of humanity, from thousands of individuals, has attached itself to these little silver spheres," he held one in the palm of his hand for illustration, "there may be some sentience, some drive for balance … I just don't know. I would welcome the challenge of finding out.

But first we should get all the balls together, a place to keep them, and see if they stay put or continue to follow us around. If they do that, I honestly don't know what we should do. It would have to be an individual undertaking."

Bob tossed the sphere to me. "What do you think?"

I held it in my hand, "It's warm … and getting warmer." I tossed it to Damien, and he to Jonesy.

Dariant said, "It knows we are talking about it. Try all the balls. I am willing to bet they are all heating up."

We did and they were; although they reached a high point of heat, they did not burn.

We stared at each other; Bob raised his eyebrows, "Now what?"

VI

'Now what?' was easy, we did nothing. We went to bed.

The next morning, the room at the tour shop was full of silver balls. Every tiny coffin we had buried in Europe was there bearing its own cargo. Also, there were dozens upon dozens of other silver balls, far more than our small group could have saved during the war.

"Apparently," spoke up Bob, "we weren't the only ones saving foil balls.'

"And what?" said Jonesy, "now, they all decide to come together?"

I asked in desperation, "What is going on?"

Darient made a guess. "It appears that something triggered the energy from all the people contributing to the foil balls. Because you were investigating, your group became the focus." He picked up a single sphere, held it, then tossed it to me. "See, they're still warm. My guess is all of them are. Something is building and will happen ... probably soon."

Darient closed his eyes and thought for a minute; the rest of us remained still. Then he spoke, "Damien, does the Poe House have a basement?"

"I," stammered Damien, "I don't know."

"You'll need to check," continued Darient, "the quicker the better." The rest of you, gather up all the spheres, in and out of boxes; don't leave a one. You need to get them to the Poe House ... fast!"

The rest of us looked blankly at him. Darient really hadn't even been one of us, yet he seemed to know what was going on and there was a command in his youthful voice that was not to be denied.

Bob spoke up, "Jaime, Jonesy, Damien, go! We'll do as Dariant says as quick as we can."

***

Beneath Damien's Poe House, down winding, narrow, first concrete then stone stairs was a round room, walls of polished and packed soil. It was dank, musty and humid. There was no light and we carried lanterns. Having brought the aluminum balls, as well as an assortment of tools (no one knew what we would need), the room was pretty much filled. Before us on the floor, in the center of the room, was an old and ornate metal door.

The room was heating up due to the heat from the silver balls as well as the tension radiating from four human bodies. Dariant had disappeared in Gettysburg, and Bob said we needed to go on without him.

"We need to hurry," muttered Bob.

"Don't suppose you have a key to that door, Damien?" I had to ask, seeing the ancient padlock.

Bob said, "Don't worry, I always have a key," as he raised a pickax above his head and brought the pick down directly onto the lock. It burst open.

"Jaime," shouted Jonesy, "get that door open!"

It took the four of us to get the door up and over, and it dropped with a loud crash. Within was a pit. A dark, seemingly bottomless pit. Damien threw a large stone into it, and we waited for a sound which never came. He said, "I always wanted to do that … but I really had hoped for a sound."

"Quick," ordered Bob," in with the balls." We did, throwing them in by the boxful, the handful, and individually, until they were all gone but one.

I told the others, "I would like to keep mine … it means a lot!" I tried to explain.

"I know," said Bob, "but it has to go with the others. What is going on here is larger than the four of us or any one person who ever collected the foil. Something is happening and we have to do our part."

I nodded and dropped that last tinfoil ball into the pit. Smoke, steam, and some hot cloudy substance began to spin up and out of the pit.

"Quick," said Damien, "the door!"

It took all or us to raise it and throw it closed. Smoke continued to seep up around the door and the temperature was quickly rising.

Bob said, "I think we need to get out of here!"

We did! Up the stairs we ran. The heat and smoke followed. When we reached the living room, the house was shaking … no, it was breathing. The walls seemed to bend in and out.

"Out!" cried Jonesy.

We ran out to the lawn and to the road. The house was emitting swirling smoke; it was black and red, and purple and orange in the outside daylight.

The cloud seemed to engulf the three-story house and the walls still seemed to be breathing, in and out, pushing deeper in and farther out with each breath. It was hard to see with the swirling cloud. The only sound was the house itself, as it flexed its beams and gables.

The colors swirled and swirled, seemingly faster. The house, almost lost from view, continued to move, suffering through its breathing agonies. Suddenly everything was still. Gradually, the mist dissipated. We could see that the house was gone. The neighboring houses still stood on each side. The mailbox was there, but there was not a board or a trace of the Poe House. All that remained was a great hole in the ground. At the bottom was a round aluminum floor, a silver surface sealing whatever had once been.

Just then in a cloud of vapors Poe's face appeared and just like that it was gone!

"I think our foil plugged the pit," Damien said after a prolonged silence.

"Something was trying to come out … I think," said Jonesy.

I said, “I think I want to go home.”

Bob quietly agreed, “Yes, go home. These things are strange and always require time and thought. As for myself,” he smiled to himself, “I have work to do.”

“Guys,” said Damien glumly, “uh, that *was* my home.”

Then he brightened, “actually, I still have the insurance money from the condo in the bank. I can buy another home. Maybe, I’ll go someplace west … far west.”

As they started to walk away to their cars, they all saw it, there on the ground was a bunch of Blood Red Roses!

D Everett Newell & Doug Hodges

Simple Pleasures

Seeing a stone skim, rippling water
Watching an eagle take flight
Looking at deer grazing in the sun
The emerald green waters of the Caribbean
Walking into a bakery, waft of smells
Feeling the summer's warm breeze
Talking to a dear friend
The PA hills in all their glory
My favorite sports team gaining a win
Silence at times can be a boost
Coffee in the AM awakens me
Watching ocean waves break on rocks
Camping out with family and friends
Music, music, concerts and more
These are all simple pleasures
Experienced and enjoyed
I'm a simple person,
I truly love all of those
Basic simple pleasures

D Everett Newell 1/14/2022

Simple Prayer

God, I kneel before you
Taking a very deep breath
Praying for all,
Especially those close
Please make their life better
Protect all of us from illness
Watch over as we sleep
Protect from as much
Of the Evil,
In this world as you can
Wash away the horrors we may see
Help us understand painful losses
Give a sign of life hereafter
March daily steadfast beside us
Holding our hands warmly, yet firmly
I do not wish this so much for myself
But want all I know blanketed
With an assurance for a good life
Long-lived, goals reached
Love, companionship achieved
These are truly the riches of being alive
Ponder my requests then, please
From my simple prayer

D Everett Newell 1/31/2022

Sitting Here

I force a smile, that I
Just can't sustain
Many dark thoughts
While I'm sitting here
Forcing smiles, hiding tears
Searching my mind's files
Thumbing the pages of my soul
Memories of good times, aide
Still many dark thoughts
While I'm sitting here
Forcing smiles, hiding tears
Memories flash by fast
But the one I need
Is not readily found
Still many dark thoughts
While I'm sitting here
Forcing smiles, hiding tears
Depression is real, devil's deal
Rays of light now clusive
Still many dark thoughts
While I'm sitting here
Forcing smiles, hiding tears
Holidays are on me, as I think
Summer sun must come fast
Trying to chase away the dark thoughts
Forcing smiles, hiding tears
While I'm sitting here

Forcing smiles, hiding tears
While I'm sitting here

D Everett Newell 12/08/2021

Most of us fight some level of depression at times, Holidays can be the worse, just don't let it beat you, reach out you're never alone!

Slang and Expressions

As I try and explain
Our written or spoken
Language, its nuances
Become so much noise
Good luck, I think, 'break a leg'
What or how is this good luck?
Hopefully our slang makes sense
In PA we 'rid up the house'
'Fill in your ideas to the blanks', you'll figure it out
'Hold your horses', slow down
'I wish', patience in explaining this
'Kitty corner' the house sits
'No meowing necessary', I promise
'Youinz is about to be taught'
Phraseology you've never heard
Our way to express
Changes regionally from
East to West, North to South
So, enjoy the trck
Flavors of our people
Not any way a measure
Of thought, It's simply
Who we are, passed down
Through generations, as my
Papa always said, 'You can teach
A horse to go without water
But he'll up and die on you!

D Everett Newell 12/12/2021

Sleepy

This AM I'm sleepy
Not of Seven Dwarfs fame
But in a fog, now alert
Got up, did my AM ritual
But when I step on the gas
I have no power, none
Sitting here in a fog
My eyelids feel like heavy blinds
With sand undertones
I hate feeling this way
And I never understand the how or why
This looking through a tunnel
Mystifies and angers me as I think
Looking for a way out of my morose
But this AM, no answers found
I'll stumble through my day
Trying to act intelligent
As if I'm here
Fighting as my ship sinks
Searching for something to jolt me
Did I tell you, this AM I'm sleepy?

D Everett Newell 8/30/2022

Slip Away

In a lifespan of an aged person
How many minutes, hours, days
Have I fretted away
Idle thoughts to no purpose
Mortgaging my life without notice
My wish would lie unfulfilled
To cash in the thrown away for now
Spending more time with those
People, events, that really mattered
In the end, I'll shed a tear
Maybe many, as even now
A salty liquid runs down my cheek
Lesson of life seldom learned
Until it's too late, I urge all
Don't let the sands of your hourglass
Slip away, without spending them begrudgingly

D Everett Newell 2/11/2023

Small Town

Eighteen, it's a hot putrid summer
Working two jobs, many hours
Very little weekly pay
Yet resilient and ready
The time now served
Saturday a rare day off
The week softball games now history
Finding time for music, girls
No schedule really, just running around
Having fun, best time to be alive
Rolling out of bed,
Enjoyed a quick shower
Shaved off my light stubble
I'm off till whenever the day ends
Best buddy picks me up
The beginning of unknown promises
Driving a two-seater
A small red convertible
Off we go, just riding around
Looking under every rock
For any and all unknown excitement
Local haunts, nearby villages
Feeling so alive, later we grab
Our two motorcycles and again take flight
One red one green two wheel chariots
Riding till dark as the cool winds prevail
Meeting up with our local gang of misfits
As our usual, off we drive to
All the local bars and live music

Anywhere within a four county boundary
Somedays I could not take it all in
Now it burns in my memory
Even thou some Sunday mornings
I may not have remembered
The excitement, laughs, my friends
Small town, with our large group of fun

D Everett Newell 10/21/2022

Dedicated to Dave, Mike, The Woodies and so many more that were drawn into our eclectic group at any time

Smart Phones

I'm proven dumb every day
Each noise the thing omits
Calls me, "Hey Stupid"
As I try to figure out
What each ringtone means
I answer "Hello" at my texts
And "call" to send one
I get so mixed up
Seeing flashing messages
Rattle by nonstop
This confounded device
Never stops, it never stops
Now I have a matching watch
Don't get me started
Spending half my days
Trying to pair and match
A new millennial dance
How in the hell
Do they call these Smart Phones?

D Everett Newell 5/6/2022

So Much Noise

Hearing a song, as it washes over me
Fills me with delight
Hearing a song as it washes over me
Helps me make it through the night

Songs, a musical interpretation of souls
The lyrics live within my mind
Songs, a musical interpretation of souls
Allow emotions to build, none left behind

Music binds me to my better past
I live again and again
Music binds me to my better past
All I've shared immediately let in

Melodies so enchanting, sometimes haunt me
Love abounds upon each note
Melodies so enchanting, sometimes haunt me
But always need them, so glad they wrote

D Everett Newell 12/16/2021

Something for this Sunday

Dreams

Yes, I was soundly asleep
A rest for the ages, dead to our world
But lately I enter a new realm
On this particular night
I walked on water, yes I did
Beneath me aqua-green liquid
Seeing fish of every size and color
Sensing the presence of sharks
Whales, manatee and more
A wondrous new world
Literally laid at my feet
Afraid I would fall in
Walked with a purposed shuffle
Increments each time, eyes wide open
Always want these dreams to last
Mostly better than our real world
No troubles, no hate, no ugliness
Nowhere in sight, nowhere in this world
Then I awoke with a smile
My heart, my soul replenished
Thankful for these trips
A voyage solely in my dreams

D Everett Newell 6/11/2023

Sometimes When

Sometimes when the wind blows
Stiff, pure, fresh, upon me
I can smell the scents of life
Flowers blooming, sure to please
After an early morning rain
The air's freshness moves me
Or holding a newborn puppy
Has an air never to be forgotten
Baby powdered babies give that
Renewal, the beginning of life
In the kitchen fresh baked bread
Or fruity pies, make my mouth water
Bacon, bacon, bacon, wow
My nostrils flaring, which
Demand an arousal to my whole being
The ability to identify much
Starts with a healthy nose
A vivid memory pulls it together
With a faint chilly draft and
Sometimes when the wind blows

D Everett Newell 3/30/2022

Song

The melodious noises
Residing in my heart
Are of many shapes, sizes
Loudly they bang, although
Intently, silently they change me
Assimilating within my soul
Stands a whole other me
Gracious, passionate, empathetic
My hardened outer shell
Melts in this warm
Vast vat of emotional soup
Both lyric and music
In this combined poetic sound
Move my mental focus
With a physical motion
Like an addiction
This partnership is trusted
To always placate fears
Enrich my happiness
Simply stated, I would be
Lost in a world without song

D Everett Newell 1/6/2022

Soul Full of Gold

Sitting, letting the music play
Watching a kaleidoscope of pictures
Pass on by, refreshing my mind
Memories taking steps as if on parade
Now an older man, but so glad
I've had the time to travel
Sharing so much I love with all
From the silly mundane, to tears
Thankful for this trek we are on
You've made my life whole
The pieces you added are soulful gold
Not ready for it to end
Yet I know the finality in sight
Still eighteen at heart, I'll go on
Till something ends my light
Hoping you'll join me as long
As you can, hand in hand
We share these breaths
And moments as only we can
Saying "I Love You" not enough
Thanks only partly true
Know the pieces you've added
Make my Soul Full of Gold

D Everett Newell 10/12/2022

Steak Sub

Love my meaty sandwich
Piled high, most eat it with
Peppers and onions sauteed
Piled on high and juicy
My mouth waters on the thought
Me, I like a Pennsylvania twist
On a toasted submarine roll
So crispy, light, buttery, brown
The steak is layered on one side
Applied next, lettuce then a layer of thin tomatoes
Now the onions join this ride
For a trip of delight
Mozzarella cheese, mayo, steak sauce
Finish it off, arriving to my lips
Piping hot, regal, and abundant
Looking forward to eating
My next steak sub!

D Everett Newell 1/8/2022

Stick and Carrot

I'm afraid days of ownership are gone
Growing up, I got rewarded, praised
While doing things the right way
A carrot if you will
The times I messed up, at school
Home, in fact anywhere, I got the stick
There was a form of accountability
Lines to not cross, rules to follow
Today an ever-escalating erosion
Of this simple life balance
Is changing our world for the worse
We do not need new rules, or laws
We need consistent punishment
For braking mandates set forth
To keep "We the People" safe and prosperous,
Got to get it back, you mess up
A measured punishment is awarded
When you do right, enrich our world
All life has to offer opens up
There are no shortcuts, nothing free
Being a true mandate for all
Simply said, value is what you give and earn
Let's get back to the stick or carrot
Methodology of doing our business
Simple, effective, orderly lives
Safer streets, schools, stores
Starts at home with all of us

D Everett Newell 2/25/2024

Summer Thoughts

I see the bright green trees
Bending to and fro in the wind
Early summer is here, I hear
The birds sing their song
This time of year smells different
The cut grass, the grills cooking
People are friendlier, lighter
It's easy being happy in June
Filled with promise, much to enjoy
Friends are dusted off, put on parade
My soul, my heart are one
At dusk the frogs and crickets align
A canopy, a cacophony of sound
Stars bursting through moonlit skies
What a beautiful world it can be
I'm almost 70 now, thinking
I will miss this as time moves on
Can't help but wonder
Will this be my last summer
Who really knows, just soak it in
Like the 68 before, smile
Cry a bit, wipe off the tears
Then repeat each day to awake

D Everett Newell 6/3/2023

Sun Shone Down

As the sun shone down
My heart emerged from its shadow
A lightness made my step easier
Fogs in my mind cleared
The path before me worn, well-traveled
Confidence building throughout me
Birds called out in symphony
Hearing small animals dart to and fro
Nature's dance being my partner
Loving days like this, an evolution
A solution to beating the blues
Warm air touched my being
Heartily I drank the tonic in
Forests and mountains fill me
With memories of years past
Wanting each beautiful moment to last
This world can give us so much
Just a willingness to explore
Opening that door, letting us out
We let all of it in, as we begin
As the sun shone down
My heart emerged from its shadow

D Everett Newell 10/21/2022

Survived

When we first start our trek
Not knowing where
Exactly our road
Will take us
Now looking back
I went as it was destined
Through childhood, teen, young adult
Miles piled up, yeah there were bumps
The potholes, cliffs were avoided
Some did wrap us up in their chasms
We fought on, this was hotly won
You see, we are survivors
If reading this up till now
Alive, standing, memories banked
You are a survivor, life's grand plan
A personal puzzle as you continue
To look then position, piece after piece
Taking shape, a tapestry unique
No two alike, each wondrous
Intrinsic to value – Congratulations!
Hand in hand we stand
Tomorrow will again come
Yesterday always you will own
You, I, we, survived!

D Everett Newell 11/17/2022

Tap on My Foot

Do signals get sent
From another dimension
In time of need
Do our spiritual loved ones
Send us clues, as to the support
They still give us
Coming to us from that great expanse
Beyond any comprehension
At six, my Granddad died
Yet the morning after
He sat upon my bed, warmly comforting
I had no fear, only felt basked in his love
After my divorce, an event
Rattled me, when both my Mom and I
Heard my son, who was not present
Say, “Hey Dad”, puzzling us
Things happen that can’t be explained
I suppose you can rationalize it all
Still, I wonder, then I ponder, puzzled
Do some of us see or hear,
Things that are amplified
More than others; do we possess
An extra sensitive antenna
This morning, half asleep
I felt this distinct four tap’s
Stern, yet loving, a warmth emitting
A light drum on my foot,
Clearing my head, smiling, I woke up

D Everett Newell 3/14/2022

Love you, miss you MOM, hope you like this

Teardrop

As I heard the Hermit sing
My mind wandered away
To the days of youthful exuberance
Swaying to the rocking beats
Laughing, smiling,
With the crowd, being one
No hatred or violence to be found
A simpler time, the one I belonged
Reality has a way of becoming forefront
Pushing through that door of memories
Then with a hard bang, closing it
Coming back to the here and now
The crowd of yesterday changed
Older, frailer, more stressed
Seeing canes, walkers, wheelchairs
The lit match sticks
Replaced by electronic cell phones
The sweet blue smoke haze
Replaced now by a mild liniment smell
My heart both felt good and pained
The joy in this night, very needed
And yet I could not stop
A large, determined teardrop

D Everett Newell 7/18/2022

Dedicated to my loving friends and my generation who enjoined Herman's Hermits Concert 7/15/2022

The Madman Cometh

At daybreak it began
The flashes, the flames
Knocking innocents out of bed
Hell on earth rings your bell
As if Hitler has risen again
Fear lights on hearts of all
People were not looking for conflict
Just wanted their daily lives
Caring, loving, going about
But no, it was disallowed
A Russian king decided their path
No freedom now
Thrown into uncertainties
Minute by minute,
They are now forced to live
No clear path forward
Except full capitulation
Waving a white flag,
No choice, one of surrender
Please Gods, protect the Ukraine
As again the madman cometh

D Everett Newell 2/24/2022

The Threads of Time

The threads of time
Woven from our yesterdays
Patch the holes
In our human sweaters
Healing as they do,
Lending new perspectives
Meeting old friends,
Ones not forgotten
Maybe on a shelf gathering dust
But time has separated,
A fresh renewal is in today's air
Filling both heart and soul
With shared emotions an entwined past
This way, making us more whole
Wonderful is our magic enjoined
Yes, something familiar reawakened
We are so very grateful
Always take the initiative to do
Rather than putting off
No tomorrows are promised
We only have today and yesterday
Thank our Gods as we do,
Awash, in this light of enjoyment
Taking note that the threads of time
Woven from our yesterdays!

D Everett Newell 3/25/2023

Dedicated to Kathy who is renewing old friendships showing me a new way

Thru Maggie's Eyes

Let me introduce to you
A wonderful furry four-legged girl
Beautiful little lady
Wearing a shimmering black coat
With a white under belly
And highlighted by brown splotches
Her life had a bad start
One day, showing up on a doorstep
Her and puppies abandoned
Luckily, the story gets better
K-Nito of Great Heart loved her
Protecting her and babies
Keeping her out of harms way
Till a flight north to Jennifer
Who again loved and supported
And found a good home for her
Thats when we
Met our new daughter
She is bright, mischievous, very playful
Everything is a game to chasing
Mommy down the hall
Grabbing at ankles,
or waking Dad up every morning
With a bevy of kisses
Loves to grab hair scrunchies
Or anything that gets us to notice
Chasing her sister Zoey is a sport
Not sure the appreciation is returned

Her love, lifts and fills us every day
With joy, making our world right
I can't ever explain why
She was given up on
But we are so thankful
They did, and she belongs to us!
I can attest
To this very important fact
The world is now a joy thru
Maggie's Eyes

D Everett Newell 11/29/2022

Together

I miss you my darling
Our house always empty
When you are gone
You are the heartbeat
Of our existence
Waiting till you return
through our door
Life is on hold
Knowing the moments bettered
For all the lives,
That you touch
Maybe you're not a super-hero
But a damn close second
So glad our paths crossed
A long, long time ago
Can only thank you,
Till our next time-then again
You'll fulfill my hopes and dreams
Glad you're always here with me
And promises that always I know
We continue to spend our time
Together

D Everett Newell 7/25/2022

To our significant others, friends, family who always brighten our lives by just being together

Toll for Thee

Many tolls in life
Many not seen, or realized
There is one from daily stress
Possibly a failed marriage
The bullshit one must put up with
At work, in public, at home
They jump on us everywhere
And at any time, no real warning
Mostly not even sensed
Our inner workings get fried
Nerves, stomach, soul rewired
Aging us without provocation
You can't fight the unseen
We just motor on
Humans are wired that way
Day upon day after day
They mount up and change us
Know you're not alone
Most sharing in this lust of living
Always remember this golden rule
Especially when being contrary to others
A toll for thee is one for me

D Everett Newell 5/27/2023

Total Eclipse

The big buzz all around
We are expecting a total
Yes, total eclipse of the sun
April 8, 2024, it will happen
Tickets are being sold,
Believe it or not
For prime viewing areas
I mean, it's the sun, same one
We can see from everywhere
On a clear bright day, it burns bright
Claiming 100,000's of people on their way
To view this spectacle, amazing
My plan, to sit in my driveway
Look towards the sky, oh yeah
With my personal ISO certified
Special eclipse lenses, I thought
Maybe I'd sell seats and parking
But seems silly to charge for this
The universe and God giving for free
In any event, I'm ready for the void
Loss of light for minutes
A lightbulb goes on, thinking
Now, I should charge to sit
In my darkened closet
No need for glasses
Each time unique
Did I mention to tell you
The big buzz all around?
We are expecting a total
Eclipse of the Sun

D Everett Newell 3/2/2024

Traveling Spirits

Would we ask entities
Of the paranormal realm
To travel on command, by request
Could this remotely be possible
That would be an intelligent haunt
But would we who dabble
Be made up of the same IQ'S
I think if spirits exist
They lay where we find them
Now I'm not omitting the tag-along
As we come into their areas
Attaching themselves to our energy
Possibly following us home
I neither believe nor disbelieve
Looking for some kind of proof
Of their existence, I'm all in
Please understand we can't schedule
A time or appointment for a ghost party
Beware of the fake conjurers
Who try to convince us
On their command, at any outing
Making a entity or being, dance
An army of traveling spirits

D Everett Newell 11/26/2022

Turning Back the Clock

If I could rewind the clock
Going back years
As I do,
Getting my swagger back
Losing my aches and pains
Going from the bald
To my youthful curly locks
A sprint now in my step
But looking around, my kids
My grandkids, evaporate
Wife now gone, I sit alone
Memories lost are now a void
All life's sorrows camouflaged
Hidden until tomorrow
Yet the good things
My achievements, my loves
My family, friends will need rebuilt
Won't ever be the same
Having a choice, I won't act
Can't risk all that has been good
Knowing the pratfalls I've been through
I'm in a good place, no need
In turning back the clock

D Everett Newell 4/30/2023

War

He never talked about it
I did not understand
How a God-fearing man
Dealt with going to war
He never talked about it
I did not understand
When he was silent and sad
From reliving the fight in his sleep
He never talked about it
I did not understand
When he did not want to leave home
He smothered us with love and protection
He never talked about it
I did not understand
At times his nerves were shot
And tempers flared, then felt bad
He never talked about it
I did not understand
Not liking the Army jacket I wore daily
With the American flag and peace symbol
He never talked about it
I did not understand
I cry now, realizing I let him down
My loving, caring, man of faith, Father
Who needed to talk about it
I now understand

D Everett Newell 1/24/2024, Jan 24th my Dad's Birthday

Water

I love watching a body of water
Lake, pond, river, or ocean
The energy it spawns
Beautiful, exciting, treacherous
Fools us at times, with calmness
Yet strong undertow is hidden
Much like our life, what you see
Is not always what you get
Like the smallest pebble
Causing a much bigger ripple
As we skim that stone off its surface
We need its sustenance to live
Up to 90% of a human body
Is made up of this renewing liquid
Water is a force, strong yet amendable
As I march through life beside it
I will go through life with admiration
I will go through life respecting
Everything and all, that is
Water!

D Everett Newell 12/02/2021

We Got Broken

When people you're close with disappear
For any number of unknown reasons
Leaving more questions than answers
From super close to strangers
Something happened, hard to explain
We got broken
Growing up sharing all, like brothers or sisters
We got broken
How did we fail each other, hard to quantify?
We got broken
Did I say the wrong thing, if so what
We got broken
My actions somehow drove you away, explain to me how
We got broken
When people you're close with disappear
For any number of unknown reasons
Leaving more questions than answers
From super close to strangers
Or simply did you just outgrow us?
We got broken
Puzzled in introspection of events and actions past
We got broken
I think of all we've missed that could have been shared
We got broken
Anyway, we had a good run 'til a split
We got broken
I sit the last three decades searching for answers of how
We got broken!

D Everett Newell 9/16/2022

Two friends I spent so much of my years from 16 to 22, always together, I'm sure you've all experienced something like this somehow the relationship crumbled when we got broken

Weeping

Have you ever
Cried yourself to sleep
Have you ever
Cried yourself dry
Have you ever
Worried yourself sick
Tossing, turning, all night long
Weeping brings red eyes
Does not solve life's ills
Have you ever
Been scared to get a doctor's prognosis
Have you ever
Been scared for a loved one
Have you ever
Just felt lost, lacking focus
Tossing and turning all night
Weeping brings red eyes
Does not solve life's ills
I know this merry-go-round
We still can't help ourselves
Being human it is our condition
Guess I'll spend amounts of energy
Dealing with issues while weeping

D Everett Newell 1/27/2022

Weight

To lose or not to lose
Begs this question
Fighting this battle is hard
Fraught with roller coaster
Ups and downs, success and failure
Go hand in hand
The soreness and aches in my
Many body bearing joints
Are a great indication
Of the downs
The freedom and painless
Movements are signs of the ups
I ask then, why is it not easier to lose the gain
Anyway, I remain on this
Front line, fighting my
Archenemy, weight

D Everett Newell 12/2/2021

What Is Beautiful

The smell of a newborn baby
Is beautiful
A fawn frolicking in a dew-laced yard
Is beautiful
See a nest with mother robin busy
Is beautiful
Hearing your very favorite song
Is beautiful
Going and experiencing a vacation
Is beautiful
Being with family and friends anywhere
Is beautiful
See the sun bringing forth a new day
Is beautiful
Seeing same sun saying a burnt orange goodnight
Is beautiful
So much in this world
That is miraculous, astounding
Things every day taking our breath away
We are very lucky to be here
I'm thankful I can share with you
My ideas of what is beautiful

D Everett Newell 6/4/2023

What is Sexy?

Very attractive
Very knowledgeable
Very confident
Very passionate
Very compassionate

Comforting
Consistent
Credible
Counted-on

People love being around you
People find you to be humorous
People find you mature
People like your innocence
People need and use your strength

You see, many things can be beautiful
You see, it's a complex blend
You see it, then you know it
You want these types in your life

Some things to me that define
What is sexy!

D Everett Newell 1/28/2022

Who Shook the Snow Globe?

Rising this morning
To the latest winter wonderland
Snow sits upon all
Manmade or nature, all covered
Trying to stay warm, dry
I look out my window perch
A nice cup of hot coffee
Watching what little traffic
Appears, disappears in my front
A person here, over there
Breaking out heavy wide shovels
The two-cylinder engines
Of many local snow blowers
Sing in unison, their January song
We traveled this path many times
Heavy snowstorms aren't new
Awed by their pristine white
Alarmed with their encompassing power
I have one question
Who shook the snow globe?

D Everett Newell 1/17/2022

Wide Awake Nightmare

I sit here late morning
Feeling dead inside,
Numbness encapsulates me
TV on, people outside moving along
Life moves about around me
Guilt fills me each time I remember
My Mom's last two years
Continually, always, 'Can you take me home?'
Albeit my dad's last words to me, as well
I could not, there was no way, Mom no longer
Had any ability to care for herself
Would not, could not, stay with us,
We tried; Lord knows we tried
Then anger, tears, fright, more anger
Reasoning on any level was used up
She needed 24/7 care
A level of care we could no longer give
Today she is gone, she is gone
Every corner I see her image, hear her voice
I can't take her home, ever again
See, I'm awake, but trapped in a visceral hell
Yes, I sit, awash in thought
One more wide-awake nightmare

D Everett Newell 3/23/2022

We all loved you so much Mom, we made decisions those last days in your best interest, God Bless you forever more!

Wipe Your Tears

When I'm gone, remember
The moments we shared
Laughs we heard, tears we shed
And when I am, the reality is
I live within all of you
The stories you'll tell
Our places you'll go
Enjoy all past and present
In my name, forge new trails
Live as I wanted you to
Taking risk, enjoying adventures
Nothing ever too small to be wondrous
Too plain to be mundane
Every moment can be special
Absorbed, each experience becomes
Layer upon layer of camaraderie
Which aides you in the darker times
Remember the light always shines
More brightly when magnified
With love and a humble approach
To all within your life's bubble
So then, please when I am gone
Remember our moments
Those special embraces
The silly things that happened
Every laugh we had, and more
Importantly, the tears we shed
Time now to wipe away any tears
Open your eyes to the future, move on
Promising I'll be there always in the
Recesses of your soul
Holding your hand at every step

D Everett Newell 7/29/2023

Woke

I awoke the other day
Not from a night's sleep
From a perception or perceptions
Of my life now and future
Looking back at a path
Well-worn, fulfilled mainly
Subjectively
I plan a trek to tomorrow
Pausing,
I wonder how many steps to go
Most of my miles used up
Wanting to now make each count
Any direction I go, I do it
With purposeful vigor, strength
Doubts creep in, can I win
Youth, vitality, not on my side
A mind, brain soiled with fog
Yet a soul that burns bright
Remains, driving a huge heart
Wanting to make our world better
In the tiny increments I can
So now, as our media chimes in
I guess you'd Color me woke

D Everett Newell 6/14/2022

Wonderful

When first noticed attraction
Sparking an unknown flame
Naive the first time
The chemistry is both
Intriguing and alarming
My body and brain short-circuit
Even feel a bit nauseous
But some connection happened
As if a plug went into an outlet
This feeling foreign, but yet
Feeling alive, no denying its power
Gloriously I followed my heart
Hoping it was not my imagination
Then I see it, a smile, yes
A positive sign from my soon-to-be mate
Taking my hand, human contact
Butterflies, nerves, stammering
It is right, I know this
Locked into each other's eyes
Leaning in, what is happening
Our lips melt into one
I am now feeling wonderful

D Everett Newell 12/10/2022

Worn Slippers

When I awake, after the bathroom
I head to the kitchen table
It is there my morning takes flight
Grabbing that piping hot cup of java
Plugging in my eyes to the world
Grabbing my watch, I get ready
But not quite yet, my feet
Are left but something wrong, unguarded
Resting on our cold floor
Then a safe harbor within reach
I pull them toward me
Slipping them on, warmth, softness
Ready to take on this day
Fighting whatever and how many
Demons may approach me
I'm set, a start, a beginning
Let my world unfold to me
As it must with anticipation
Grinning, I sit back, as the
Last piece of this ritual completes
The wearing of my worn slippers

D Everett Newell 5/2/2022

Would I… Wondering

Sitting in my room
I'm 16 or 17, many thoughts
Sweeping over me,
Insecurities of youth
Wondering how the finished me
Would turn out, anxious years
Playing record after record
The long playing vinyl
Spinning round and round
Much like the thoughts in my head
Questions really of
Life and the future
Would I ever own a home?
Maybe a woman would marry me?
Kids? Would I leave
That lasting legacy?
Now I look back, realizing
That it was all for naught
My life took the path it did
One that was predestined to be
Mostly happy,
Mixed with some tragedies
Like anyone's life, no more
Than I could bear,
I'm still here
But never do I question anymore
Would I?

D Everett Newell 11/11/2022

Write

I'd write anywhere I could
I'd write by using pencil
I'd write by using pen
    By the light of the sun
I'd write using coal
I'd write using chalk
I'd write in blood
    By the light of the moon
Nothing will stop me writing
Not a storm, loss of power
Dim lights, or noisy rooms
When passions hits, words
Come fast and furious
From chasms deep within
Much like a sneeze
Almost involuntary, I must
Yes, I must write!

D Everett Newell 12/16/2021

W.T. Grants

U.S. Grant was my favorite Civil War general
W.T., I do not believe was related
William Thomas had a grand idea,
Of having many branded store items
Offered in the same space, one stop shopping
His chain flourished through the 1960s, mid-1970s
I came in 1971, this is my story

Hired part-time about thirty hours a week
Five to nine nightly,
Usually, eight hours Saturday
During the holiday seasons, nine to one pm Sunday
I'd be many things during my sojourn
Mainly a Men's Dept salesclerk
Back then, we were expected to help customers,
Know our products

On weekends, I branched out, staffing the Toy Dept
And on Sundays I opened the doors,
Oversaw the restaurant
Where you could find the best 'all you can eat Fish Fries;
And where my high school crush,
Became my first serious relationship

At times I played Santa
Which was a rehearsal for my next job, at Fisher Price Toys
Where the motto was, "Our work is child's play"
Child's play was great for my next occupation,
At the Eastman Kodak Co.

D Everett Newell 12/16/2021

Yes, Yes, Yes

Yes, Yes, Yes
I say to all
Of the rainbows after rains
The clean smell of little babies
Yes, Yes, Yes
I say to all
Of the snowcapped mountains
And the rivers waterfalls
Yes, Yes, Yes
I say to all
Planning, then going on vacation
Watching a puppy as it frolics
Yes, Yes, Yes
I say to all
Seeing big white fluffy snowflakes fall
Sitting by a roaring toast fire
Yes, Yes, Yes
I say to all
Yes, Yes, Yes

D Everett Newell 1/7/2022

www.ingramcontent.com/pod-product-compliance
Lightning Source LLC
LaVergne TN
LVHW041158150826
845673LV00001B/212

* 9 7 8 8 1 1 9 6 5 4 4 1 3 *